DEAL MAKERS

Negotiating More Effectively Using Timeless Values

DEAL MAKERS

Negotiating More Effectively Using Timeless Values

William H. McClendon, III, Esq., BA, LLB

For George W. Kuney
Many Thanks,
March 10, 2011 Bill McClendon

Bonneville Books
Springville, Utah

ISBN 13: 978-1-59955-500-3
Published by Bonneville Books, an imprint of Cedar Fort, Inc., 2373 W. 700 S., Springville, UT 84663
Distributed by Cedar Fort, Inc., www.cedarfort.com

LIBRARY OF CONGRESS CATALOGING-IN-PUBLICATION DATA

McClendon, Bill, 1933-
Deal makers : negotiating effectively using timeless values / Bill McClendon.
p. cm.
Includes bibliographical references and index.
Summary: A lawyer's handbook on how to win at negotiations by having integrity.
ISBN 978-1-59955-500-3
1. Negotiation. 2. Integrity. I. Title.

BF637.N4M385 2010
302.3--dc22

2010043710

Cover design by Megan Whittier
Cover design © 2010 by Lyle Mortimer
Edited and typeset by Megan E. Welton

Printed in the United States of America

10 9 8 7 6 5 4 3 2 1

Printed on acid-free paper

To my wife, Genie; to my children, Hutch, Virginia, Eleanor, and Bryan; and to all of my students and clients whose insights and enthusiasm contributed so much to this book.

Contents

Preface:

Seeing the Big Picture

Samuel L. Clemens (1835–1910), the Mississippi riverboat pilot who wrote under the pen name Mark Twain, was once asked by a youngster who climbed up to the wheel-house, "Sir, how are you able to be such a good riverboat pilot when it is so dark and foggy out here on the Mississippi?"

> Clemens answered, "You know, I studied books. I memorized charts and principles, practiced with equipment, learned the rules of navigation but, you know, the mighty river is ever-changing and my real training came from experience on the river itself because it is only here that I gained my sixth sense, my intuition . . . to be able to detect hidden obstructions by observing the current and the color of both the water and the bank . . . You must see the big picture and know the shape of the river, the ever-changing patterns because, when it is dark and foggy, that is all you can go by."

Clemens established a relationship with the river and discovered its purpose. This insight made Clemens a good riverboat pilot and, as Mark Twain, a great writer. In both roles, he learned the basics, filed away facts and experience for future retrieval, and saw connections among different areas of knowledge. He anticipated that, if pursued far enough, these areas make binding contacts with each other. Most importantly, he used the predictable patterns in the river. He trusted his informed intuition—approaches that apply equally well to negotiating more effectively.

One of the most profound patterns I learned was in 1986, when U.S. Circuit Court of Appeals Judge Alvin B. Rubin encouraged me to teach a course on negotiations and professionalism in the Law Center at Louisiana State University, a course he had previously taught with great success. I was teaching another course there and was particularly interested in Judge Rubin's approach to professionalism. So, you can imagine my excitement about teaching a competitive skill with emphasis on professionalism. I was ready.

"What particular book are you using, Judge?" I asked.

He answered, "There is none. Improvise from your own experience as a practicing lawyer and add a twist emphasizing professionalism."

Judge Rubin wanted professionals to rise to a higher level of consciousness. He espoused the need for attention to fairness that transcended the rules of professional responsibility. He felt that "professionals can be expected to observe something more than the morality of the marketplace" because they "cannot ethically accept an arrangement that is completely unfair to the other side, be that opponent a patsy or a tax collector."[1]

I decided then to focus on an approach to illustrate that the art of negotiation, when linked with the timeless values of professionalism, cannot be comprehended solely by deductive reasoning or analytical skill; it can only be encountered, practiced, and acquired with the negotiator mind-set. This mind-set requires focused listening, innovative strategy planning implemented through appropriate tactics, and sound decision making, skills that are not inherited but must be acquired over a lifetime of patience and practice.

What is the best way to describe this link that exists between the ethical force of timeless values and the competitive force of the negotiator mind-set? Thinking about this over the years, I wondered whether timeless values follow certain unchangeable patterns just as mathematics, science, and nature all appear to be out of one unchangeable constant. Is it not in our ethical practices that the principles of timeless values are stored and maintained?

No matter how far we might attempt to be relevant to the modern world, if we keep one foot in these ancient teachings, we are pulled back, time and time again, to the tried and true. It is to these enduring principles found in timeless values that every age looks. This is how and why timeless values add trust and, consequently, enhance negotiation effectiveness.

Just as the spiral symbol illustrates an unchangeable ratio existing throughout nature (from the smallest spiral seashell to the largest spiral galaxy, including our own Milky Way), so can it represent the enduring force of timeless values. When we link the competitive force of the negotiator mind-set with the ethical force of timeless values, we achieve our goal located between, and as a result of, these two forces, which is to negotiate more effectively. With one force, we focus on a disciplined toughness and a determined will to sense the situation and out-think our opponent. With the other force, we focus on adhering to timeless values—particularly courage, loyalty, civility, tolerance, truthfulness, compassion, persistence, and integrity—that form the very foundation for professionalism.

Business traditions may change, but values do not.[2] Being more persuasive in our business, professional, and private pursuits requires that we become vastly more intuitive. We are better able to recognize repeating patterns in the negotiation process, to review facts as curious explorers for hints as to how things are not quite what they seem,[3] and to examine knowledge critically to see if it still fits.[4] We increase our awareness of links among different areas of knowledge. We learn to grab the novel ideas that interest us the most, and we combine them with our own unique experiences. We develop a determination, the negotiator mind-set, which includes a determination to make the deal. And, as Judge Rubin suggested, we add a twist of professionalism to our methods. The result of Judge Rubin's challenge and my years of working with these ideas is this book. I am still moved by the potential of its message. Enjoy!

NOTES

1. Alvin B. Rubin, Judge, U.S. 5th Circuit Court of Appeals; Professor-Adjunct LSU Law Center, *Teaching Legal Negotiations,* 35 LLR 577 (1975), 578–79.
2. This phrase was used by the Southern Strategy Group in

the December 2009 edition of The Baton Rouge Business Report.

3. Adopted from Steven D. Levitt and Stephen J. Dubner, *Freakonomics: A Rogue Economist Explores the Hidden Side of Everything* (New York: HarperCollins Publishers, 2005), X.
4. Phrase used by award winning, Stacy Overstreet, "Excellence in Teaching" in *Tulanian* (Fall 2002).

Overview:

Integrating the Components

Deal Makers discusses ten closely related components that structure an effective negotiation process and consequently form a negotiation module that integrates ethical principles of professionalism with disciplined toughness of the negotiator mind-set. These ten components may be considered in any sequence (even backwards) because they are closely related chapter concepts and not separate steps. Therefore, they should be reviewed only as part of a dynamic whole.

Part I—Beginning the Process directs attention to the lens through which we view the negotiation experience, the predictable patterns in the negotiation process, and the basic rules of the game.

Part II—Becoming More Skilled emphasizes active listening with four ears, strategy planning, tactical maneuvering, and using the mediation open-ended question as a negotiation tactic.

Part III—Being More Persuasive focuses on the subtlety of signals in communication, the classical art of persuasion, and timeless values—the key ingredients of professionalism.

Notice on the following concept chart that from top to bottom, the negotiation process starts with patterns and rules, adds skills, and ends with affirmation of timeless values. Moving across, the result of this process is an effective negotiator who has both integrity and technical expertise. Also notice the coalescence of our two forces: the ethical force of timeless values found in professionalism and the competitive force of disciplined toughness found in the negotiator mind-set.

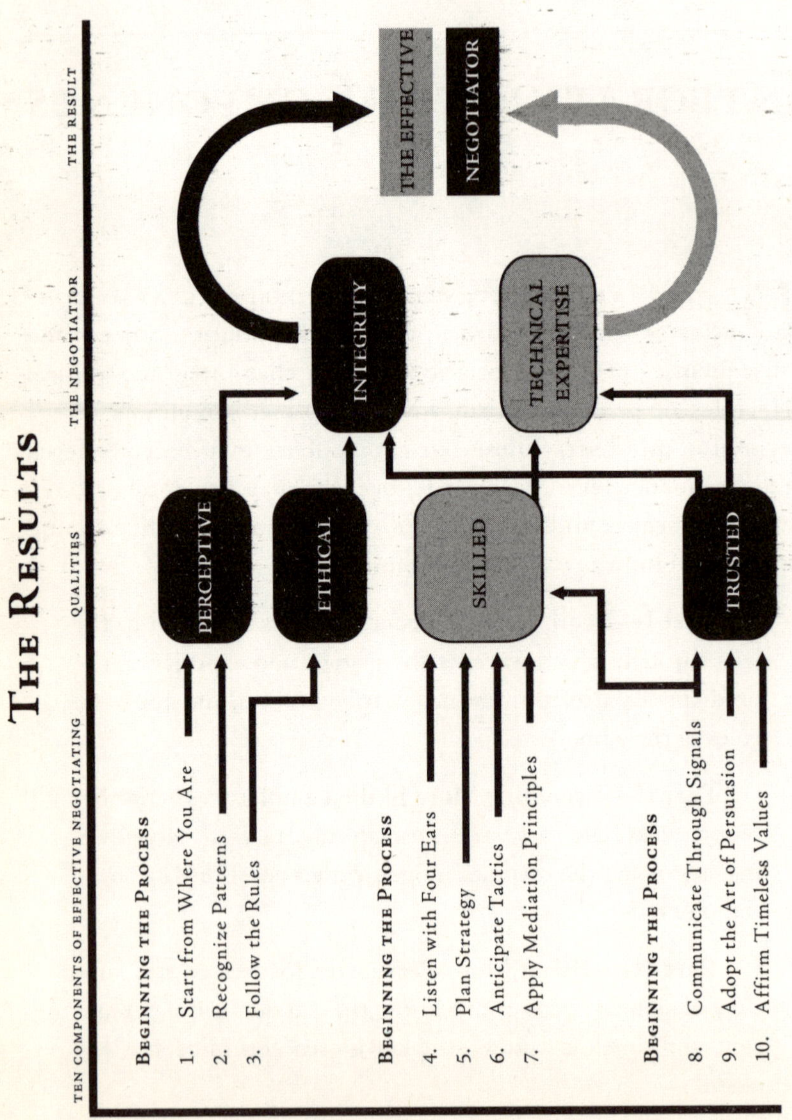

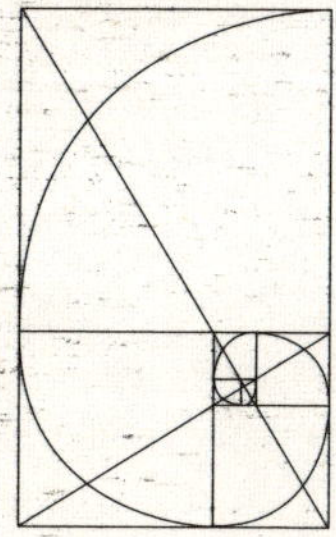

Part I: Beginning the Process

Component One:

Start from Where You Are

Determining What Added-Value to Offer

TRUST IS THE OPENING CALL BEFORE THE CURTAIN GOES up. The negotiation drama is awaiting. We look forward to using our persuasive skills as negotiators. But first, we seek insight by answering these questions: "Where do we begin our quest to determine what added-value to offer? How do we recognize the predictable patterns in the negotiation process? What do we need to know about the basic rules of the game? What do we stand for as individuals?"

Is our tendency to use primarily the left hemisphere of our brains to focus on being sequential, logical, and analytical? Or do we make a conscious effort also to use our right hemisphere for nonlinear, intuitive relationship-building and seeing the "big picture" approaches? These "right brain" qualities include inventiveness, empathy, joyfulness, and meaning and "increasingly will determine who flourishes and who flounders. For individuals, families, and organizations, professional success and personal fulfillment now require a whole new mind."[1] Increasing our creativity as problem-solvers requires us to be aware of our problem-solving process and to be ready, when necessary, to update our well-developed thinking style in order to avoid conceptual blocks to our creative thinking. We must use intuition and feeling as well as reason and logic.[2]

We also must be aware of the effect of purposeful power used over people and its lever—force, wealth, and knowledge. In Japanese legend the sources of power are represented by the sword, the jewel, and the mirror.[3]

At the beginning of every negotiation, we must consider an important question: what added-value do we bring to the table as negotiators—knowledge, expertise, professionalism? This preliminary consideration is not something that gets in the way but is the way that leads to negotiating more effectively.

INSPECT PERSONAL LENSES

Our focus begins only in one place: where we are right now, as we explore what we are and what we might become. This is a good time to clean our reading glasses with soap, as my wife says. We must ask ourselves: "What images do I have about negotiating, and where did I get them? What is this personal lens through which I see everything? In other words, Where am I coming from? Where am I heading? What choices have I made that most influence who I am today?" These everyday questions hint at a larger question: "What is my story?"

Successful negotiators point out that they see negotiations through the lens of professionalism. They assert that there is a need to go beyond the minimum standards to professional values, which provide guidance when negotiators are neither required to nor prohibited from doing something by disciplinary or legal liability rules but have the freedom of choice to abide by a higher standard.[4]

Professional choice is not an abstract concept existing by itself. We will always be known not by our knowledge but by the choices we make. Establishing respect for and trust in ourselves as negotiators are requisite for mastering the classical art of persuasion.

An old friend and fellow lawyer once wisely advised, "Be careful and don't let the practice of your profession change your personality."[5]

Using Tolstoy Wisdom

In reflecting upon the War of 1812 and why people burn houses and destroy their fellow man, Leo Tolstoy (1828–1910) points out that consciousness is a source of self-cognition quite apart from and independent of reason. Through his reason man *observes* himself, but only through consciousness does he *know* himself. He considers himself outside of time because he measures flowing time by the fixed moment of the present in which he alone is conscious of his existence. Just as the early belief in the immovability of the Earth was overcome by the acceptance of motion that man does not feel, so man must recognize that a complete freedom of personality does not exist but is heavily influenced by outside factors of which he is not conscious.[6]

Applying Oz Insights

The Wizard of Oz is one of my favorite stories. It was written by L. Frank Baum over a hundred years ago, and made famous by MGM in 1939. Four characters go to the City of Oz in hopes of finding solutions to their lives' concerns: a Tin Man, searching for a heart; a Cowardly Lion, courage; a Scarecrow full of straw, brains; and Dorothy, who is sure that the solution to life lay in just walking far enough.[7]

As the Wizard speaks to the group in a commanding voice from behind a curtain, Dorothy's dog, Toto, pulls back the curtain, exposing the Wizard. Dorothy tells him that he is a very bad man. He replies, "Oh no my dear; I'm really a very good man; but I'm a very bad Wizard, I must admit." But the Wizard is a worker of profound change. He is a man who can watch, listen to, and perceive others as they really are:

- **The Scarecrow** doesn't have any brains, or at least thinks he doesn't. He sees other people who seem to get things done so more quickly, who make better grades, and who always have the right answer.
- **The Cowardly Lion** worries not so much that he doesn't have brains enough to make a plan but that he doesn't have enough courage to do it.
- **The Tin Man** is afraid he lacks compassion and feeling because he doesn't have a heart.
- **Dorothy** is looking for security and safety. She wants to feel more comfortable. She wants to go home.

All negotiators have in them a little bit of the Scarecrow, the Cowardly Lion, the Tin Man, and Dorothy. But what does the Wizard do? As Frederick Buechner points out in a commencement address, the Wizard turns out to be a very great wizard indeed because he has X-ray eyes to look beneath the surface to see what the four are afraid of and who they really are. The Wizard gives the lion a medal of courage, the Tin Man a heart-shaped locket to hang around his neck, and the Scarecrow a diploma to show his intelligence. The Wizard, in the end, brings forth in all of them the magic they already had. This provides profound insight in the search for identity that all negotiators experience. As Dorothy witnesses what happens to her companions, she herself gains more self-confidence and is more comfortable.[8]

Sharing Insights

Sharing insights with students across multiple disciplines—law, engineering, accounting, and business—from various countries—Canada, Nicaragua, Colombia, Brazil, India, China, Pakistan, Turkey, Germany, Albania, Lithuania, and Ethiopia—is one of the most cherished aspects of my teaching. Several of these students serve as plant managers and business executives. Their insights (shown throughout the text as Insights from a Fresh Perspective) give us a snapshot of how a new generation of negotiators from both Western and non-Western cultures think and feel.

> ***Insights from a Fresh Perspective:*** *An African parable states: "Every morning in Africa, a gazelle wakes up. It knows that it must run faster than the fastest lion, or it will be killed. Every morning a lion wakes up. It knows that it must outrun the slowest gazelle, or it will starve to death. It doesn't matter whether you are a lion or a gazelle; when the sun comes up, you better be running." Determine whether you are the lion or the gazelle, consider how far and how fast you have to run to make it home, pace yourself, and try to enjoy the journey. Recognizing what role you are to play instead of what you are afraid you are can make the road home a bit easier.*

CREATE CONNECTIONS

In considering new concepts, our awareness of links among different fields of learning increases, creating connections that often become pathways to new solutions. In the 1986 movie *Top Gun,* Tom Cruise plays Maverick, a fighter pilot trainee. His instructor asks him what he would do if attacked by an enemy MIG from one o'clock.

He must ask himself whether to give "the textbook answer" or "the right answer." He answers that he would do a hard bank to the left, roll, and swing around behind the MIG. The instructor says this is, according to the book, the wrong answer because of excess pressure to the wings. Later the instructor acknowledges that Maverick has intuitively discovered a new solution and, in actual combat, could do this maneuver safely, perhaps saving his life. Likewise, negotiators can call up stored information to exercise, on the spur-of-the-moment, what is really needed: creativity and good judgment. This involves knowing intuitively when to press, when to back off, when to make the final offer, when to recess, and when to stop.

> ***Insights from a Fresh Perspective:*** *Just like negotiation, jazz improvisation requires preparation. Musicians study tunes, chords, and music theory for years. Once a jazz musician takes the stage, he has to stop thinking about theory. He has to completely rely on his intuition to reproduce what he has previously learned, because at heart, music is about expressing emotions. When emotion is effectively communicated through music, the piece becomes personal and unique. Good negotiation is like great music; it has to be personal and unique to be appropriate and thereby successful.*

Focusing on Face-Giving and Feelings

Feelings are facts, and sometimes they are so important they must be dealt with at the beginning of a negotiation. Feelings involve the heart, and sometimes the heart has its own reasons of which our rational mind is not aware. The heart feels what the mind cannot grasp. Feelings often involve saving face. Face work should focus not on the strategies we employ to save our own face but, more importantly, on how we save the face of the other person, which is a process known as face-giving. Remember that different cultures react differently. For example, people in Asia, Africa, and Latin America are predominately "collectivistic." They focus on preserving the social status of the in-group. People in the United States, Canada, and Western Europe are more "individualistic," operating from an outcome-oriented model. A collectivist acknowledges the other's concerns and obligations toward the in-group. An individualist, on the other hand, engages in explicit verbal acknowledgment, recognizing the individual names, faces, abilities, and skills of the other.[9]

In the 1991 movie *The Doctor,* starring William Hurt as Dr. Jack MacKee, a group of medical students scurry behind a doctor who turns and shouts, "All right, what you have to do is learn to cut, and cut straight, that's all. One shot to go in and fix it. What is the diagnosis here? What is the remedy?" A few days later, this doctor, diagnosed with cancer, is put in the hospital. He undergoes five months of treatment and has a miraculous recovery. He returns—a little thinner, a little grayer—to his class of medical students, holding in each arm a bundle of green hospital gowns.

"Tomorrow morning at 8:00, everyone in this class is going to report to the hospital. You have been given an 'ailment.' You are going to stay in the hospital two days and receive all of the tests that are assigned for that ailment. After two days, this class will resume."

When the class resumes, he stands up before the class, "You have spent a lot of time learning Latin names for the body parts of your patients. But patients have names and feel frightened, and they have put their lives in our hands. We must learn a patient's perspective. Good luck!"

The movie ends with the doctor reading a letter from a young girl who has just died of cancer. She tells him how to attract birds and animals and then says, "Let down your arms, Jack, and we will all come to you and be relaxed."

> ***Insights from a Fresh Perspective:*** *Perception is reality. It is imperative that our perceptions are free from limiting factors such as bias and pride. Hans Christian Andersen's children's story* The Emperor's New Clothes *illustrates this principle beautifully: the king's pride blinds him from seeing that he is being swindled, and his people's conceit leaves them unable and unwilling to identify the fact that the king is not wearing any clothes. It is my role as a negotiator to be free from prejudice, to be the only one who sees the situation as it actually is, and who cries out, "But he has nothing on at all."*

Using Positive Emotions

Emotions play a powerful role both in our capacity to perceive and express feelings as well our ability to engage in clear thinking. Positive emotions enhance relationships, which, in turn, greatly increase the potential for problem solving. A negotiator should: 1) express appreciation and recognition for valued contributions made; 2) build affiliation or a sense of connectedness with the other; 3) acknowledge the status of the other's social or cultural expertise; and 4) develop roles, which are fulfilling.[10]

> ***Insights from a Fresh Perspective:*** *Sometimes in negotiations, your opponent's stance seems as absurd as that of the anxious news reporter who stands out in the middle of a hurricane. As a professional negotiator, however, you have a duty both to understand your opponent's reason for acting in what may seem like an illogical manner and to try and persuade your opponent to "come in out of the rain," and see your side. Turning an adversary into a partner can make a difference. It could make a hurricane-like negotiation seem like nothing more than a gentle rain.*

Just as a little more weight can increase the stability of an arch, adding more meaning to a negotiation can increase insight. The more meaning interjected into a situation, the more focus there is on fulfilling that meaning. Psychologist Viktor Frankl said, "You should try to live as if you were living already for the second time and as if you had acted the first time as wrongly as you are about to act now."[11] To gain a better perspective on the possible consequences of a decision, step back and imagine evaluating the situation as if the decision had already been made.

Reducing Tensions

When we feel pressured by artificial deadlines, we need to rise above the resulting tension. As we move from regular mail to airmail, to special delivery, to telegraph, to fax, to email, to text messaging, we must realize that there is a tendency to take less time to think—to give a considered reply. Some point out that there is also a growing tension because we tend to look to our own resources for solutions rather than seeking the advice of others and that the Internet age has caused "a steady devaluing of expertise," where "experience is downright suspect."[12]

The successful negotiator must focus on maintaining a healthy self because we all harbor many conflicting tendencies. We know we are part beast and part saint, a mixture of folly and reason, love and hate, courage and cowardice. And the coexistence of these conflicting traits naturally causes tension.[13] It is then even more important to be kind to ourselves because of this tension. "If you are not your own best friend, then who is? Have you ever caught yourself doing something right—how about approximately right?"[14]

> ***Insights from a Fresh Perspective:*** *The tea ceremony is a part of Chinese culture, which can be dated back some 4,000 years. Green tea (called "true" tea with real leaves) is the unique type, baked immediately after picking with no fermentation process. Besides all the health benefits, it has long been considered a symbol of living tranquilly without seeking fame and wealth. It is perfect at the negotiation table in China. Negotiation is not always a win-lose game. In business, it is more often the case that mutual benefit leads to future cooperation. The tranquility of the natural green color, the cultural background of green tea, its unique transparency, freshness, and delicate fragrance leave negotiators free to think and feel more deeply with calm and content mood.*

INCREASE CONTROL

Increasing control of the negotiation process often requires changing the style or approach used to fit the circumstances.

Choosing a Style

Our negotiation style is an important element in determining what we stand for and what value to offer. But style generalizations by themselves are seldom helpful.

ADVERSARIAL: (WIN/LOSE SITUATION)—"a kind of warfare." Objective: to win and win fast by beating the opponent. "Winning isn't everything—it's the only thing."[15] A high degree of determination is needed. Well-tuned aggressiveness with decisiveness often tips the balance of power. Courage is needed to allow risks, as well as self-confidence to limit them when risks are unwise. Remember that the negotiator never has to be belligerent to be aggressive; being tough doesn't mean being rough.

cooperative: (win/win situation)—"a problem-solving process." Objective: to build a relationship while seeking mutually satisfactory solutions. This style requires determination and courage similar to the adversarial style. The negotiator needs some aggressiveness to hold high aspirations and to stay focused to achieve them. The potential for finding joint gain (it can't be divided until it's discovered) is far greater than most negotiators realize.[16]

combination: (cooperative and adversarial)—Objective: to be versatile, and adopt either style convincingly with the right combination of assertiveness and toughness. A certain amount of tension always exists, regardless of style, between cooperative moves to create value and competitive moves to claim value.

Practical Tips

Since no single negotiation approach works best in all negotiations, the negotiator should use a variety of approaches and styles and know when to choose each. It has been shown that competitive tactics early in the negotiation sometimes increase the prospects for successful use of cooperative or problem-solving tactics later in the negotiation.[17]

While cooperative and aggressive negotiators tend to bring out the worst in each other when they are on opposite sides of a problem, they bring out the best in each other when consciously working together on the same side of a negotiation. Gerald Williams points out that, in many negotiation competitions, the negotiators sometimes find themselves switching roles. The negotiator assigned to be aggressive may recognize, for example, that his or her cooperative partner has suddenly become very aggressive, and will switch to a more cooperative point of view as a counterbalance to the unexpected aggressiveness of the partner.[18]

The mutual gains approach is neither completely hard nor soft, but rather is both hard and soft with emphasis on interests

> and needs of the parties rather than positions. The method of principled negotiation developed at the Harvard Negotiation Project is to decide issues on their merits rather than through a haggling process focused on what each side says it will and will not do. Parties learn to look for mutual gains wherever possible, and, where interests conflict, to insist that the result be based on some fair standards independent of the will of either side. This method of principled negotiation is hard on the merits, soft on the people.[19]

Incorporating Different Approaches

There are two main approaches to negotiation:

Principled Negotiation employs a mutual gain or interest-based approach. It involves identifying the underlying interests and needs of the parties, creating a range of alternatives and options, and focusing on improving the working relationship between the parties. Sometimes the pie to be divided is enlarged, benefiting both parties.

Positional Negotiation, on the other hand, models zero-sum bargaining, determining simply how much one party will win and the other will lose. The pie is viewed as being only so big, and it cannot be divided in a way that one person receives more without the other receiving less.

DEVELOP A COMPETITIVE ATTITUDE

One of the few things over which we as negotiators have total control is our attitude. We need to reserve the greatest respect for ourselves, for it is what we perceive ourselves to be that often determines our quality of life.[20] We need to develop qualities of mind that people value the most in professionals: common sense, creativity, good judgment, and a sense of competency and control, not to control others, but to be able to do successfully what we set out to do.[21] This involves adopting a negotiator mind-set and expanding the informed intuition. This also involves feeling the momentum increasing so that we seek not to become someone different, but rather, a stronger version of ourselves.

not just today's ride, but getting halfway to lunch, or to the next rest stop, or even to the next turn. Second, have a positive attitude. Focus on the stuff you don't like, and you will be miserable.[22]

Adopting a Negotiator Mind-set

The negotiator mind-set is similar to the mind-set found in competitive sports. This mind-set is both relaxed and intensely focused.[23] It liberates the conscious mind so it can fully and innovatively zero in on the "hard analytic skills" of critical thinking and logical reasoning.[24]

This state of relaxed concentration has long been recognized as a basic element in high performance under pressure. It is similar to the approach of world champion tennis players. They practice their game so that they can use their best shots when they are needed most, without having to consciously think about them.

So what does "trust yourself" mean in tennis? It doesn't mean positive thinking—for example, expecting that we are going to hit an ace on every serve. Trusting the body in tennis means letting the body hit the ball. The key word is let. We trust in the competence of our bodies and brains and let them swing the racket. Then, when we go out on the court, we have "no magic phrase that must be repeated, and we can concentrate without thinking."[25] There is a similar lesson in golf. Here, the ability to concentrate is good, but thinking too much can be disastrous. We must trust our muscles and hit the ball to the hole. Keep it simple.[26]

Expanding the Informed Intuition

Our problem-solving skills as negotiators sometimes rely heavily on our ability to inform and use our unconscious minds, our intuition. In some ways, our informed intuition can act as a "coach." We create a database with our coach so vast and varied that answers are available "on call" for a large variety of circumstances. In his book *Blink,* Malcolm Gladwell states that learning to control instinctive judgments and first impressions dramatically increases a person's power of knowing what to do in the first two seconds, in the "blink of an eye," and we that can be empowered to make "quick, accurate, intuitive decisions."[27] The secret to using our unconscious more effectively is to recognize it. "The more creative thinking is done, the more natural and rewarding it becomes and the more the ego relaxes," according to another author.[28]

Sometimes it is helpful to think of our informed intuition as a source of whimsical, out-of-the-box hunches, ideas, and visual images, which might relate to the negotiation challenges at hand. Our unconscious mind is freed up to engage in more creative thinking and imaginative problem solving.

For me, the informed intuition is like a "back-burner" where great ingredients simmer to become well seasoned. For example, when I cook a tasty beer-based sauce for grilling chicken, I add the lemon juice, lemon peels, mustard, green onions, olive oil, beer, and seasoning, and then allow the ingredients to simmer on the "back-burner" for the purpose of developing their full taste. I do not rush the process. Like the negotiator, I do not pay a lot of attention to the exact measurements of the ingredients or to how long they must simmer (or to how many drinks I consume while cooking). I just "know" when the sauce is ready. All knowledge is linked, like the ingredients in a good sauce.

Experienced negotiators point out that understanding what we stand for as individuals is useful in evaluating what others do or don't stand for and how contrasting values send signals, and operate to direct a negotiation through the informed intuition. For example, "a person who values a 'win/win' outcome may have to convert an opponent who values a 'win-at-all-cost' approach before any real progress can be achieved."[29] Remember that what lenses we use to look through and what particular style or approach we choose form predictable patterns in the negotiation process, a topic we will consider in our next component.

Can you identify a pattern in your negotiating?

Summary

- Trust yourself and the negotiation process.
- Prepare to offer added-value.
- Remember, you will be known not by knowledge, but by the choices made.
- Remember, character forms trust, the prerequisite for persuading.
- Use positive emotions to enhance relationships.
- Look for ways to reduce tensions.
- Practice using your informed intuition so that it is trained and developed like other skills.

NOTES

1. Daniel H. Pink, *A Whole New Mind: Why Right-Brainers Will Rule the Future* (New York: Penguin, 2006), 3.
2. James L. Adams, *Conceptual Blockbusting: A Guide to Better Ideas* (Reading, MA: Addison-Wesley Publishing Company, 1995), 59.
3. Alvin Toffler, *Power Shift: Knowledge, Wealth, and Violence at the Edge of The 21st Century* (New York: Bantam Books, 1991), 13, 14, 15.
4. Adopted from a discussion with Professor Carl Pierce of the University of Tennessee College of Law.
5. Gordon F. Wilson Jr., attorney, New Orleans, LA, speaking to the class.
6. Second Epilogue of Leo Tolstoy, *War and Peace* (New York: Simon and Schuster, 1942), 1347, 1351.
7. Loren C. Eiseley, *The Unexpected Universe* (New York: Harcourt, 1972), 123, 124.
8. *Westminster Bulletin* (Westminster School, Simsbury Conn. 1987), 1–3.
9. Eric van Ginkel, "The Mediator as Face-Giver" in *Negotiation Journal* 20 (October, 2004), 475–487. Van Ginkel is adjunct

professor in alternative dispute resolution at Pepperdine University School of Law and international counsel at Hughes Hubbard & Reed LLP.

10. Roger Fisher and Daniel Shapiro *Beyond Reason: Using Emotions As You Negotiate* (New York: Viking, 2005), 28–36, 53, 54, 95–111, 117–133. Additional ideas found in: Erin Ryan, "Building the Emotionally Learned Negotiator" in Negotiation Journal 22 (April 2006), 209–225.
11. Viktor E. Frankl, *Man's Search for Meaning* (New York: Pocket Books, 1985), 131, 132. Frankl was a world-renowned psychiatrist and neurologist from Vienna who endured years of unspeakable horror in Nazi death camps.
12. Matt Bai, "What Does it Take," in *The New York Times Magazine* (July 15, 2007), 16.
13. René Dubos *A God Within* (New York: Scribner, 1984). 84, 85.
14. Kenneth H. Blanchard and Spencer Johnson *One Minute Manager, 2nd Ed.* (New York: HarperCollins Business, 2000), 38, 40, 41, 78.
15. Joel Sayre. "He Flies on One Wing." *Sports Illustrated*, 3.26 (1955, Dec. 26), 48.
16. Gerald R Williams, *Legal Negotiation and Settlement* (New York: West Publishing, 1983), 24–25, 41–42, 49.
17. Donald G. Gifford, *Gifford's Legal Negotiation Theory and Applications* (New York: West Publishing, 2001), 133.
18. Gerald R. Williams, *Legal Negotiation and Settlement* (New York: West Publishing, 1983), 41–42, 49.
19. Roger Fisher and William Ury, *Getting To Yes: Negotiating Agreement Without Giving In, 2nd Ed.* (Boston: Houghton Mifflin, 1992), 10–12.
20. James E. Rohn and Ronald L. Reynolds, *Seasons of Life* (Southlake, TX: Jim Rohn International , 1981), 32, 49, 50, 52.
21. Gerry Spence, *How to Argue & Win Every Time: At Home, At Work, In Court, Everywhere, Everyday* (New York: St. Martin's Griffin, 1996), 47, 65.
22. Bill Jacobs, *From Sea to Shining Sea on my Bicycle*, (Cashiers

Crossroad Chronicle, October 27,2010) 1B, 10B

23. W. Timothy Gallway, *The Inner Game of Golf*, (New York, Random House, 1981), 21, 26, 49, 80, 96, 104, 117, 206.
24. Idea adopted from Robert M. Lloyd, "Hard Law Firm and Soft Law Schools," in *North Carolina Law Review* 83 N.C.L. Rev. 667 (2005) Professor, Tennessee College of Law, commenting on the recent book by Michael Barone, *Hard America, Soft American: Competition vs. Coddling and the Battle for the Nation's Future* (New York: Three Rivers Press, 2005).
25. W. Timothy Gallwey, *The Inner Game of Tennis*, (New York: Random House, 1974), 51. The development of inner skills requires learning to control the mind and to concentrate the energy of awareness, 21.
26. Harvey Penick and Bud Shrake, *And If You Play Golf, You're My Friend: Further Reflections of a Grown Caddie* (New York: Simon & Schuster, 1999), 52.
27. Malcolm Gladwell, *Blink: The Power of Thinking Without Thinking* (Boston: Little, Brown, and Company, 2005), 15–16. For a clearer understanding of the corollary principle, see Gladwell's earlier book, *The Tipping Point: How Little Things Can Make a Big Difference* (Boston: Little, Brown, and Company, 2000).
28. James L. Adams, *Conceptual Blockbusting, A Guide to Better Ideas* (Addison-Wesley Publishing Company, MA, 1995), 129.
29. Comments on this section by Leon Gary, Attorney, Baton Rouge.

Component Two:

Recognize Patterns

Using the Negotiation Process

The present computer age supplies us with endless information. But to be truly effective as negotiators, we must develop our negotiator mind-set, find the innovation to grasp the great ideas and recognize the patterns present. We look for these repeating patterns in the negotiation process without being blinded by pattern-thinking. This is an empowering concept. Patterns exist everywhere for all of life's experiences, particularly for negotiations. Remember that it is not the "stuff" out of which something is created but the "patterns" that exist inside that stuff that are so important.[1]

Routines, actions, rhythms, shapes, colors, tastes, and feelings all hint at underlying patterns that awaken thought. This gives us great insight and the ability to anticipate. But we need to be careful about making too broad a generalization or becoming so fixed in a given pattern of thinking that we become paralyzed and unable to think creatively. We must seek an understanding of the opponent's reasoning and the patterns that exist in that logic in order to anticipate the next move.

Many negotiation ideas are well understood by people of experience—but understood in the world of practice, and not in the world of thought. Practitioners often act intuitively in ways that are far more sophisticated than they can conceptualize and articulate. Leading scholars point out that even these sophisticated practitioners can profit by contrasting negotiations in their own field with those in others, and by reflecting about what pattern lies within the common core.[2]

We now shift our focus to the interaction patterns jointly created in the discourse between two negotiators. In this way, we better visualize the patterns in which the parties communicate to ensure that they understand each other. This communication has a jointly constructed meaning rather than separate statements. We locate meaning in the sequence rather than in the utterance. Recognizing these patterns helps us anticipate how the actions we take are likely to be interpreted, and responded to, by the other.[3]

Benjamin Franklin wrote that experience is a dear teacher, but fools will learn in no other school.[4] Many negotiators pride themselves on learning only by experience, but the wise ones also study theory because theory incorporates the experience of many in the form of new knowledge.[5]

Practical Tips

While negotiation, intuition, and experience are irreplaceable tools, they become much more useful if harnessed by an overall conceptual framework.[6]

EXAMINE INTERNAL MAPS

The lens through which we view negotiations shapes how the pattern of the negotiation process will be interpreted. To focus just on negotiation techniques and tactics is like cramming through school: we make the deadline but never achieve true mastery of the subject. While we might work on behavior (try harder, study more) or improve our attitude (think positively, hold down emotions), we may still be lost if the wrong pattern is being followed.

Looking for patterns involves drawing distinctions. This in turn allows us to see more sides of an issue. We create new categories, we become more open to new information, and we sense different perspectives. All of this greatly improves our thinking and leads to better understanding.

Ever notice how much easier it is to look through a grove of trees to a pasture while moving rapidly down the road instead of standing still? The human mind is constantly extracting sensory experiences and organizing them so that selected bits of information enable us to view existence as a continuous whole. In a sense, the mind creates an internal map showing a pattern, but the map is not the territory. The value of the map is derived from its relationship to the territory. The greater the similarity between maps of different people, the greater the shared understanding. This ability to examine our lenses and internal maps is especially helpful in dealing with ethical and moral issues embedded in the details, like trees along the road that block our view.

Wrestling with Ethical Issues

Ethical values are effective in making moral choices because they increase awareness of situational factors that skew our better judgment. It is good cause to think about how others have wrestled with ethical and moral issues. Are there patterns present from which we can learn? What ethical considerations caused these men and women of history to react the way they did? To gain insight as to what course we, in similar circumstances, would choose, we must ask ourselves a series of questions about the circumstances surrounding a particular decision: "What type of ethical principle or moral value is involved? Is it a choice between two moral values, or between a moral value and an immoral act? What would I do in a similar circumstance? Is there a difference between what I think I should do and what I feel I should do?" As we try to absorb these lessons from the past, we should emotionally commit to those ethical principles that both our intellect and heart choose.

Gaining Insight from Others

The comments of three famous negotiators, separated by over 2,000 years, are pertinent: Cicero (43 B.C.E.); Machiavelli (1515 C.E.); and Professor Roger Fisher (present). Each wrote extensively on this subject, and although they don't always agree, their approaches illustrate the power of recognizing ethical patterns.

Cicero[7] As a Roman Consul and Senator, Cicero was committed to the restoration of the Roman Republic following the assassination of Julius Caesar in 44 B.C.E. He used the question well, and he was eloquent and forceful as a speaker and as a writer. In one letter, he tells his son that no immoral act (in politics or elsewhere) should ever be expedient because certain universal laws arise from man's own soul and nature and reign supreme, even above Roman Law. Qualities like honor, courage, fairness, truthfulness, and integrity are such basic principles of character that self-subordination to these principles, far from confining a person's ability to succeed, would enlarge it. This, in turn, would lead to strength of spirit and good judgment.

During the civil unrest that followed Caesar's assassination, Cicero persisted in being outspoken against anyone wanting to become emperor instead of restoring the republic. He asked difficult questions as he spoke in the Forum about Mark Antony:

> Do you suppose that when men would not put up with Caesar, they will put up with you? Believe me, they will compete with one another hereafter as they run to do this work. Come back to your senses sometime, I beg of you; think of those from whom you have sprung, not those with whom you live. Deal with me as you will, but come back into the good graces of the republic.[8]

A few months later, Mark Antony killed Cicero and nailed his head and hands to the speaker's rostrum in the Forum. Years later, Mark Antony, with his mistress and ally, Cleopatra of Egypt, deserted the battle against Octavius at Actium and soon after, committed suicide. But Cicero lives on through his beautifully clear writings:

> True law is right reason consonant with nature, pervading all things, constant, eternal. . . . It is not lawful to alter this law, to derogate from it, or to repeal it. Nor can we possibly be absolved from this law, either by the Senate or by the Assembly. This law does not differ for Rome or for Athens, for the present or the future, for one unchanging and eternal law shall be valid for all nations and for all times; and so it becomes, as it were, the general master and governor, the one god of all men, being itself its own author, promulgator, and enforcer.[9]

Machiavelli As a successful diplomat for the dynamic city-state of Florence, Machiavelli negotiated with the King of France, the Pope, and the Emperor Maximilian. During this time, he began an in-depth observation and analysis of national political forces. In 1512, the Medici family regained power over the republic. Machiavelli, the career diplomat, suddenly lost his job, was exiled from the city for a time, and was imprisoned, and was even tortured on the rack. Upon his release, he retired with his family to the country where he read, studied classics, and wrote in order to keep himself mentally alert and ready to re-enter diplomatic service when called. Every night he pretended to have "conversations" in his library with ancient writers, vividly reliving with the particular writer great moments in history. In his internal dialogue, he asked himself questions about the key elements of success. He collected these pragmatic observations in a small book entitled *Principles of Power* (later mistranslated as *The Prince*), which he dedicated to the Medici family in hopes of returning as their diplomat. He wrote:

> A prince ought to have no other aim or thought, nor select anything else for his study, than war and its rules and discipline; for this is the sole art that belongs to him who rules.... And again, he need not make himself weary at incurring a reproach for those vices without which the state can only be saved with difficulty, for if everything is considered carefully, it will be found that something which looks like virtue, if followed, would be his ruin; whilst something else, which looks like vice, yet followed brings him security and prosperity.... Those princes who have done great things have held good faith of little account, and have known how to circumvent the intellect of men by craft.[10]

Scholars have pointed out that Machiavelli probably was replying to Cicero in stating that political expediency is above ethics and morality sometimes and that, when necessary, a wise ruling power must use craft, deception, deceit, and cruelty as political weapons. Machiavelli was not hired by the Medici family, and when the republic was re-established in 1527, the general outcry against his book, perhaps unfairly, precluded his re-election to his former diplomatic post. His health failed, and a few months later, at age 58, he died. *The*

Prince lives on as one of the world's great books, but the word "Machiavellian" is presently defined as "subtle or unscrupulous, cunning."[11]

Fisher Professor Roger Fisher of Harvard University is renowned as a counselor to presidents, international adviser to diplomats, and founder of the Harvard Negotiation Project. He is author or co-author of many negotiation classics including *Getting to Yes, Negotiating Agreement Without Giving In; Getting Together, Building Relationships as We Negotiate;* and *Beyond Reason, Using Emotions as You Negotiate.* What is particularly pertinent to our discussion of ethical patterns is his co-authored book *Beyond Machiavelli.*[12] The great insight of this book is that negotiators like Machiavelli should ask themselves questions like, "What are the key elements of success?" and, "How can we be effective negotiators while adhering to the highest standards of ethics and professionalism?"

Professor Fisher points out that cold calculation about rational conduct and logical deduction by themselves can lead to amoral, if not immoral, actions that often look like the mechanical manipulation of others. With evil and selfish people in the world, it is wise to remember that "he who sups with the devil should have a long spoon!" Professor Fisher asserts that when generating advice, the focus should not be solely on giving answers (as education has programmed many to do) but on the process of asking better questions. This process should involve questions not leading to one-shot answers about who is right and who is wrong but a series of questions directed toward the process for dealing with differing views about what is right and what is wrong.

Avoiding Blind Spots

In thinking about what these people did and what happened to them, remember that we all have blind spots. There will always be aspects of the negotiation that we cannot see. Just as our view of the scenery is obstructed when standing behind a big white pine or live oak, we are unable to see the reality of our situation because of our blind spots. Timeless values define our profession and character and improve our vision so we can see around our blind spots.

To gain greater insight when we examine our actions, motives, and outcomes, we need to take our blinders off. We need to be aware of the fact that our action is often an anxious reaction to external factors. We may be reacting to a blind spot. But whatever the reason, we are not in control; we want to escape the power of the reflexive response. Noticing our blind spots also leads us to the realization that sometimes we may even "intentionally seek out those situations that will trigger our favored reactions."[13]

EXPERIENCE THE SEQUENCE

Experiences of negotiators fit into a pattern—there is a particular sequence which, when followed, always yields the best results.[14] Therefore, we need to study and read broadly to create a store of ideas to enhance our mental backup system of known alternatives for solving negotiation problems. This increases our personal database to become more mentally limber. We develop links to new solutions instead of stockpiling ideas we won't use.

Remember the old saying, "If you know the enemy and know yourself, you need not fear the result of a hundred battles. If you know yourself but not the enemy, for every victory gained you will suffer defeat. If you know neither the enemy nor yourself, you will succumb in every battle."[15]

Understanding the Other Side's Thinking

Understanding another's thinking is crucial to experiencing the process sequence. This is not simply a useful activity that helps solve the problem. The other's thinking is the problem because differences are defined by the differences between our thinking and the other's.[16] This requires us to think about various things at the same time. Remember the wise saying that the test of a good intelligence is the ability to hold two opposed ideas in mind at the same time and still retain the ability to function effectively.[17]

In order to better recognize the patterns in negotiations, we must artificially halt the interaction of these forces, examine them individually, and determine which forces are really driving the negotiation. The more we move inside the negotiation process to speculate about how it works, the more insight we gain.[18]

For some, it will be like learning to speak a foreign language by studying the grammar only to forget it later. Yet, when learning a new language, the studying of grammar first is imperative if we are to become fluent.

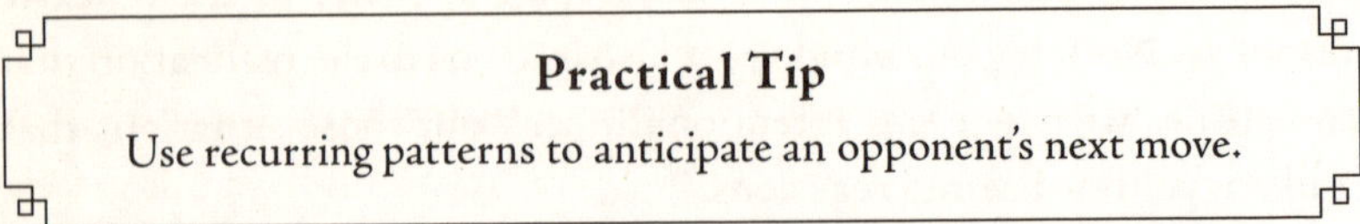

Practical Tip

Use recurring patterns to anticipate an opponent's next move.

Asking the Right Question

Vernon Porter, the cofounder of the Taylor Porter Law Firm in Baton Rouge, Louisiana, had a great sense of humor, dignity, and timing. Shortly after I started with the firm, I asked Mr. Porter about what questions should be asked of new clients. He told me what had happened to him soon after he started with the firm in 1912. The receptionist called to announce that a strange-looking man with the collar of his overcoat turned up was asking for a short conference. Mr. Porter greeted the man, ushered him into his office, and said, "When Mr. Taylor hired me, he advised that I should always first ask a new client the nature of his business." The stranger sat down, pulled out a flask, took a drink, and said, "I understand your hourly rate is $15 . . . and I figured I would have my first drink today with a good lawyer . . . let's see, I've used up about 15 or 20 minutes of your time . . . so here's $5. Many thanks." Mr. Porter loved to tell this story and end with, "You know, you must try to understand the other's thinking. I believe that was one of the hardest fees I ever earned."

TRY ANALOGY-THINKING

Analogy-thinking helps us discover relationships and gain a feel for something that cannot be adequately described in words. This includes experience with painting, music and theater; with cooking; with sports such as golf, tennis, skiing, football, basketball, volleyball, baseball, boxing, archery and fishing; and with hobbies like chess. It is important to use these experiences as opportunities to gather images, organize them, and gain new perspective by applying analogy-thinking. Like other global skills—for example, reading, driving a car, skiing, playing golf and tennis, riding a bicycle, and walking—art is made up of component skills that become integrated into a whole skill.[19] I think of this as our informed intuition.

Many of us, particularly in law, business, and engineering, have been programmed in vertical thinking, proceeding systematically from a known concept through the particular issues of the problem to a conclusion. This approach, however, frequently does not work in dealing with others. False assumptions cause us to have a built-in bias that is all the more confining because it is unconscious and obscures certain types of information. Using horizontal or lateral thinking and incorporating analogy removes this built-in bias. This is where lively minds well versed in vertical thinking strike imaginative sparks one from another.[20]

There are many times, despite innovative problem-solving techniques, where we are just not able to make sense of a situation. We don't have enough information, patterns are vague, things too complex, or we are not yet prepared. Simply looking for more patterns is clearly not enough. Pattern-watching has its limits. What do we do?

We use storybuilding by trying to connect the observed events to explain how they might have come about. In other words, we pick up patterns and fold them together to build a story. Once the story is constructed, it becomes a very powerful tool for organizing the rest of the material and for making sense of the situation. Constructing the story works like the picture on the puzzle box that tells us what the scene is supposed to look like.

This puzzle analogy, however, is not entirely accurate because the pieces of a puzzle have a fixed shape. In many complex situations, the pieces of the story often change shape. We become aware of our blind side because pattern recognition and storybuilding are of no use if we are insensitive to unexpected or novel events that we have never been exposed to. Therefore, they are not part of our mind-set. If we are not aware of this possibility, we may become so fixed in our false story that we become focused on explaining away the inconvenient facts. It now becomes increasingly difficult to have an open mind because once we construct the data (incorrectly) to justify our belief and make sense of the situation, it is very difficult to see this data from another perspective. So in all of this, we must be realistic, accept the limitations of a particular approach, be prepared to find flaws in our thinking, and stay mentally limber.[21]

Baseball

Baseball, like negotiations, gives us wonderful insight for making the most of the human brain. David Brooks of the *New York Times* stated that baseball players constantly practice their routines so that the automatic mind is better trained. This automatic mind is responsible for most baseball actions. This is why professional players have developed "phenomenal automatic brains," and why steps have been taken to keep the conscious mind from interfering. A calm, detached manner is encouraged, particularly when a player has just made a key catch or struck out swinging. An air of nonchalance ensures that the player remains steady and ready for the next play. This practical baseball wisdom applies equally well to negotiating. "It is not taught but imparted through experience. It consists of a sensitivity to the contours of how a situation may evolve, which cannot be put into words."[22]

Snow Skiing

In snow skiing, often the beginning move signals not isolated techniques or movements, but a sequence, a chain, a complex of moves that occur together, often in the same pattern, time and time again.[23] Understanding a sequence increases confidence in skiing, and in negotiations, because of the recognizable pattern.

Golf

One of the classic golf instructors of all time, Percy Boomer, explains that in golf, we never act purely psychologically or purely physically, but every act is a type of unison. When this unison is functioning properly, it provides a form of conscious control, which is precisely what a golfer needs. It is a form of control that replaces thinking. And thinking has to be replaced because if our golf is dependent upon thinking, it is at the mercy of our mental state. Excitement, depression, elation—any emotion can lead to distraction. Learning by a sense of feel is something quite different from learning by the intellect. Intellectual memory may be of use, but it does not replace a memory for the right feeling of a movement, which enables the muscles to repeat that movement time after time without directions from the brain or will. When it is said that someone has a "good golfing temperament," this means that the golfer has sufficient control to produce the best shot whatever the circumstances may be.[24]

Fishing

Fishing, much like the art of negotiating, involves a delicate process. One must patiently experiment in order to find the right approach.

> ***Insights from a Fresh Perspective:*** *My father and grandfather used to take me fishing when I was young. Both men were excellent fishermen but could not really tell me how to fish—they used to say that it was something that I had to learn on my own. I practiced and practiced until I started catching fish. I learned that you must be quiet and listen so you don't scare the fish away. I also learned that it is important to know when to use either artificial or live bait. This varies by the type of fish that you are catching and the type of water you are fishing.*

Reading

Reading is a helpful analogy because it involves making meaning and processing information in stages. The eye is like a camera, but the brain is not. The brain cannot take in the retinal images, only electric impulses. One of the problems that some people have in reading is a tendency to spend too much time trying to nail down one part before moving on. This usually causes needless frustration because there is often no way to find out what an early part means until a latter part is revealed. Since words actually contain no meaning until we read them, it is more interesting to pay closer attention to what actually happens in the mind of the reader during the process of reading.[25] Comprehension is more than simply understanding the circumstances; it is the way in which we learn. This may be the reverse of the situation where we are expected to learn in order to understand. But learning is more a result of comprehension than its cause. Experts—whether in reading, art, chess, or engineering—may be able to comprehend an entire situation at a single glance.[26]

Writing

Writing provides another helpful analogy to negotiations because it involves making choices, forming meaning, and recognizing patterns. The writer must interpret what is seen, heard, and felt. This is because writing is a nonlinear process in which the writer continually circles back to reviewing and rewriting.[27] What we are looking for influences how we seek because how we seek controls what we find.[28] In writing, we see how things are related; we form concepts, and then we think with these concepts.[29] This allows us to think about thinking, have interpersonal dialogue, learn to tolerate ambiguity, use ambiguities as the hinges of thought, and to make meaning out of chaos. Meanings are created by seeing relationships as words and ideas bring one another to consciousness. This creates purpose. The Spanish word *conscientisation* has been defined as the creative and critical use of language.[30] Reality is known not directly but by means of the meanings that we make. We need to look and look again because how we construe is how we construct. Meanings do not just happen: we make, find, and form them.[31]

Art, Acting, and Music

Daniel H. Pink, in *A Whole New Mind: Why Right-Brainers Will Rule the Future*[32], explains how the left hemisphere of the brain analyzes the details of information and how the right hemisphere synthesizes the big picture. He then very forcefully points out that what is needed to succeed today is not the ability to grasp the details (a left brain function of lawyers, doctors, accountants, engineers, and executives being outsourced to China, the Philippines, and India) but the ability to build relationships, to see the big picture, to engage in complex syntheses (a right brain function invoking the ability to create artistic and emotional beauty which uses more holistic, intuitive, and nonlinear reasoning).

Our focus in learning today should be on "using right-brained functions, such as forging relationships, rather than executing transactions; tackling novel challenges instead of solving routine problems; and synthesizing the big picture rather than analyzing a single component."[33] Only the human mind can think by analogy, can see relationships, grasp the meaning of spirituality, build empathy, and create emotions. How does this apply to us as negotiators? We should take art lessons, listen to great symphonies, go to classic plays, and think about our thinking.

> ***Insights from a Fresh Perspective:*** *Recurring patterns remind me of the use of repetition in art. What strikes me about the use of repetition is what the great designer Paul Rand called a "catalyst for surprise," which is also very useful when challenging another negotiator. If a pattern emerges in negotiation, you can completely change or challenge that pattern as a way of attaining your opponent's full attention and getting them to listen to your point of view. That "catalyst for surprise" puts them off guard and makes them unsure as to whether they have a full understanding of the situation. You then step in with a carefully crafted message to which they are more likely to pay close attention.*

Shortly before he died in 1997, Jimmy Stewart, a Hollywood icon, was asked how one becomes a great actor: "You don't do this just by reading about it or attending lectures. Acting is learned by consistently working through it—by breaking it down and not just rehearsing and reading the lines but by seeing reality through the character's perspective."

> ***Insights from a Fresh Perspective:*** *A string quartet is very different from an orchestra in how the music is guided. An orchestra uses a conductor to stop, start, and cue various parts. In a string quartet, however, each person jointly controls the music. This shared control requires each member of the quartet to listen carefully to the other three members, listening with more than just their ears. By the time the sound of another's instrument reaches your ears, it is too late to be in sync with their notes. This means that each member has to look for non-verbal cues from the other players in order to perceive the correct tempo, tone, volume, and bowing style. Similarly, by the time one hears what the other is saying in negotiation, it is too late to think proactively.*

FOCUS ON ONE THING AT A TIME

In applying a business approach to the game of golf, Ken Blanchard states, "There is always a better golfer inside struggling to get out! The trouble is, most people try to learn and remember too many things when they play: Swing! Grip! Align! Balance! Distance! The mind boggles, the brain rebels, and the shot whistles off into the rough. . . . There are some key mechanics that every golfer should know, but the main emphasis must be placed upon the relationship between mind and body. When an individual has a clear purpose, the ego can be kept under control; patience and persistence will become friends."[34]

Historic golf instructor Harvey Penick points out, with tongue in cheek, that when a person is asked to take an aspirin, it is assumed that the person will not take the whole bottle. In the golf swing, a tiny change can make a huge difference. The natural inclination is to overdo the tiny change that has brought success. So, a golfer makes an exaggerated effort in order to improve, consequently leading to confusion and loss. Penick further points out that lessons are not to take the place of practice but to make practice worthwhile.[35]

The late Charles Yates, former British Amateur champion and member of Augusta National, told me in Cashiers, North Carolina, that he once asked his long-time friend, the legendary Bobby Jones, what was best to think about when playing golf. Bobby replied, "You know, I've found that when I thought about three things, I didn't do too well—two things, and I did a little better. But I did my best when I only thought about one thing at a time."

Being Realistic

In World War II, the British Singapore fort guarded the point at the Indian Ocean and China Sea with all guns pointed toward the sea. The Japanese surprised the British by attacking through the dense jungle from the north. Spencer Chapman escaped for six months in the jungle, which was full of deadly insects and plants, where one bite or sting would kill; where dangerous animals could attack at any given moment; or where lush fruit could easily sustain life. Chapman's experience, and topic of his book, *The Jungle Is Neutral*[36], illustrates the principle that the jungle is not out to consume life nor make it any easier; the jungle is merely neutral. Likewise, our life experiences are all neutral.

Jim Collins, in *Good to Great*[37], provides two examples that further illustrate the need to be realistic. The first is about Winston Churchill, who understood the liabilities of his strong personality and compensated for them during World War II. He maintained a bold and unwavering vision that Britain would not just survive but prevail as a great nation, despite the whole world wondering not if but when Britain would sue for peace. During the darkest days, with nearly all of Europe and North Africa under Nazi control and with the United States hoping to stay out of the conflict and Hitler fighting a one-front war (he had not yet turned on Russia), Churchill said, "We are resolved to destroy Hitler and every vestige of the Nazi regime. From this, nothing will turn us. Nothing! We will never parley. We will never negotiate with Hitler or any of his gang. We shall fight him by land. We shall fight him by sea. We shall fight him in the air. Until, with God's help, we have rid the earth of his shadow."

Churchill never failed to confront the most brutal facts. He feared that his towering, charismatic personality might deter bad news from reaching him in its starkest form. So early in the war, he created an entirely separate department outside the normal chain of command called the Statistical Office, with the principal function of feeding him the most brutal facts of reality. He relied heavily on this special unit throughout the war, repeatedly asking for just the facts. As the Nazi *panzers* swept across Europe, Churchill went to bed and slept soundly. "I . . . had no need for cheering dreams," he wrote. "Facts are better than dreams."

Collins' second example concerns Admiral Jim Stockdale, the highest ranking U.S. military officer in the "Hanoi Hilton," tortured over twenty times during his eight-year imprisonment at the height of the Vietnam War, and later awarded the Congressional Medal of Honor. In an interview, he said, "I never lost faith in the end of the story. I never doubted not only that I would get out, but also that I would prevail in the end and turn the experience into the defining event of my life, which, in retrospect, I would not trade." As Stockdale continued his slow walk, limping and arc-swinging his stiff leg that had never fully recovered from repeated torture, he was asked, "Well, who didn't make it out?"

"Oh, that's easy," he said, "the optimists. They were the ones who said, 'We're going to be out by Christmas. And Christmas would come, and Christmas would go. Then, they'd say, 'We're going to be out by Easter.' And Easter would come, and Easter would go. And then Thanksgiving, and then it would be Christmas again. And they died of a broken heart." After a long pause and more walking, he turned and said, "This is a very important lesson. You must never confuse the faith that you will prevail in the end—which you can never afford to lose—with the discipline to confront the most brutal facts of your current reality, whatever they might be."[38]

Practical Tips

In the *planning phase,* research the facts, the law, and the opponent while anticipating in the mind's eye possible tactics and techniques. Assess strengths and weaknesses affecting both sides and catalog contingencies, ascertain aspiration levels, and anticipate limits and goals.

In the *preliminary phase,* establish relationships and ask questions to ascertain more facts. Observe carefully to read the tone of the interaction, whether it will be competitive (with little chance of change), or a combination of competitive and cooperative approaches.

In the *question phase,* move from just seeking more facts to looking past stated positions for signals and hints as to an opponent's real interests and needs, the target and resistance points. Be conscious of controlling disclosure of your own information.

In the *bargaining* or *distributive phase,* begin with principled positions that can be rationally explained. Then claim value, carefully control concessions, and patiently wait for the process to evolve.

In the *closing phase,* the tone shifts to be more cooperative, the size of concessions decrease, and non-verbal signals indicate an end is approaching.

Avoiding Being Blinded by Fixed Patterns

My former rector, the Reverend John Senette, tells the story of Nasrudin:

> Nasrudin used to take his donkey across a frontier every day, with the panniers loaded with straw. Since he admitted to being a

smuggler when he trudged home every night, the frontier guards searched him again and again. They searched his person, sifted the straw, steeped it in water, even burned it from time to time. Meanwhile, Nasrudin was becoming visibly more and more prosperous.

Then he retired and went to live in another country. Here, one of the customs officers met him years later. "You can tell me now, Nasrudin," he said, "Whatever was it that you were smuggling when we could never catch you?"

"Donkeys," said Nasrudin.

Unexamined, fixed patterns can blind the negotiator to viable solutions. Some negotiators are like the frontier guards who could not figure out what Nasrudin was getting past them. Nasrudin knew that their minds were so fixed on a particular pattern, they couldn't allow their eyes to see or their intellect to comprehend what was right in front of them.

Look for recurring patterns in order to predict and plan.

Summary

- Study and read broadly to create ideas and links to new solutions.
- Seek to understand an opponent's reasoning.
- Use analogy-thinking.
- Focus on one thing at a time.
- Avoid being blinded by fixed patterns.

NOTES

1. Douglas R. Hofstadter, Godel, Escher, *Bach: An Eternal Golden Braid* (New York: Basic Books, Pulitzer Prize Winner, 1999), 4, 674 .
2. Howard Raiffa, John Richardson and David Metcalfe, *Negotiation Analysis: The Science and Art of Collaborative Decision Making* (Cambridge, MA: Harvard University Press, 2002), 84, 195, 213, 249.
3. Lawrence Sunskind, *Negotiation Journal* 26, no. 117: 163–66.

4. Benjamin Franklin, *Poor Richard's Almanac,* 1743 (Philadelphia: Printed and Sold by B. Franklin, 1733), 4.
5. David Churchman, *Negotiation: Process, Tactics, Theory* (Lanham MD, University Press of America, 1995), 57.
6. John S. Murray, Alan Scott Rau, and Edward F. Sherman, *Negotiation* (Foundation Press, 1996), 43.
7. The quotes and ideas adopted from Robert Payne, *The Horizon Book of Ancient Rome* (American Heritage Publishing Co., Inc., Library of Congress Catalog Card Number 66–18667), 138, 139. See also, A.H. Clough, *Plutarch's Lives,* Volume II (NY: A.H. Burt Company), 394.
8. Ibid., Second Phillippie.
9. Ibid., Il republica.
10. Adapted from *Great Books of the Western World* (Encyclopedia Britannica, 1952, Volume 23), 21.
11. *Random House Dictionary of the English Language,* Unabridged Version, (New York, 1973), 859.
12. Roger Fisher, Kopelman, and Schneider. *Beyond Machiavelli: Tools for Coping With Conflict* (Cambridge, MA, Harvard Press, 1994), 4, 8, 107, 144.
13. Parker J. Palmer. *The Active Life* (HarperCollins Publishing, Inc., San Francisco, 1991), 38–40.
14. Maureen Berman and I. William Zartman, *The Practical Negotiator* (New Haven, CT: Yale University Press, 1983), XIII.
15. Sun Tzu translated by Samuel B. Griffith, *The Art of War* (Oxford University Press, 1963), 18. Sun Tzu wrote The Art of War circa 500 B.C.E.
16. John S. Murray, Alan Scott Rau, and Edward F. Sherman, *Negotiation* (Foundation Press, 2002), 158, 179, 189.
17. Adopted from F. Scott Fitzgerald. This phrase used in chapter heading entitled "Managing Ambiguity and Paradox" by Thomas J. Peters and Robert H. Waterman, *In Search of Excellence* (Harper & Row, 1982), 89.
18. Donald M. Murray, *Learning by Teaching, Selected Articles in Writing and Teaching* (Portsmouth, NH, Boynton/Cook, 1982), 21.

19. Betty Edwards, *Drawing on the Right Side of the Brain*, Rev. Ed. (New York: Tarcher/Penguin USA, 1989), XVIII.
20. Krome Barratt, *Logic and Design: The Syntax of Art, Science & Mathematics* (Bernardsville, NJ: Eastview Editions, 1980), 289, 290.
21. Information for last three paragraphs adopted from Gary Klein, *The Power of Intuition* (Doubleday, NY, 2003) 144–147.
22. David Brooks, "Your Brain on Baseball", *New York Times*, (March 18, 2007), 13.
23. Lito Tejada-Flores, *Breakthrough on the New Skis: Say Goodbye to the Intermediate Blues*, 3rd ed. (Mountain Sports Press, 2001), 5.
24. Percy Boomer, *On Learning Golf*, Rev. Ed. (Classics of Golf, 2007), 18, 143, 203, 207.
25. Peter Elbow and Pat Belanoff, *Being a Writer: A Community of Writers Revisited* (McGraw-Hill, 2002), 199, 200, 207.
26. Frank Smith, *Understanding Reading: A Psycholinguistic Analysis of Reading and Learning to Read*, 6th Ed. (Mahwah, New Jersey: Lawrence Erlbaum Associates, 2004), 163.
27. Ann E. Berthoff, *The Making of Meaning: Metaphors, Models and Maxims for Writing Teachers* (Portsmouth, NH: Boynton/Cook Publishers, 1981), 28.
28. Ibid., 50.
29. Ibid., 57.
30. Ibid., 92.
31. Ibid., 10.
32. Daniel H. Pink, *A Whole New Mind, Why Right-Brainers Will Rule the Future* (NY: The Penguin Group, 2006), 22.
33. Ibid., 141.
34. Ken Blanchard, *Playing the Great Game of Golf: Making Every Minute Count* (Quill, 1994), XIII, 138.
35. Harvey Penick, *Harvey Penick's Little Red Book: Lessons and Teachings from a Lifetime of Golf* (New York: Simon & Schuster, 1999), 27, 72, 172.

36. Spencer Chapman, *The Jungle Is Neutral: A Soldier's Two-Year Escape from the Japanese Army* (Guilford, CT: The Lyons Press, 2003), 5.
37. Jim Collins, *Good to Great: Why Some Companies Make the Leap . . . and Others Don't* (New York: HarperCollins Publishers, 2001), 73 .
38. Ibid., 85.

Component Three:

Follow the Rules

Accepting Good Ethics as the Basis for Professionalism

Accepting good ethics as the basis for professionalism in negotiations is our last component in Part I and forms the backdrop for our forthcoming consideration of key negotiation skills in Part II. These include listening carefully, planning strategy, implementing tactics, and applying mediation techniques. Just knowing that we are abiding by the rules of the game removes nagging concerns, increases confidence, and improves effectiveness.

CHOOSE A MORAL MAP

The role of ethical philosophy as a guide is not always clear. The main themes of classical ethics do not address what we should do when confronted with contradictory accounts of what happened; nor do ethics address what appears to be imminent. Rather, ethical philosophy raises the question of what we should do when we know what we are doing. Negotiation often involves inexact, disputed reconstruction of past events and perceptions as the basis for decisions (this circumstance is depicted by the figure of justice, who weighs the scales while blindfolded). Likewise, making sound ethical decisions poses a challenge because we have to mediate constantly between general ethical norms and actual ethical problems. Ethical philosophy, however, does have a place in professional ethics. The ideal of "justice" is real even if, in practice, it may be unattainable. Roman soldiers crossed their right arm on the chest to signify *integritas*. The ideal of "truth" is real even if, in practice, its realization is incomplete. Virtue, loyalty, courage, civility, integrity, and other timeless values all remain worthy goals.[1] Many a coach has been heard to say, "know the rules and they will help you," particularly Tommy Lasorda of the Los Angeles Dodgers.

What should words and ideas such as truthfulness, dishonesty, horse-trading, professional responsibility, justice, fair play, and honor mean to the negotiator? Teachers assert that in this adversarial system, "you can't negotiate without knowing who you are and what you stand for . . . and whether you are honorable. . . . You fly your own standard—it is on your own shield—and people will know."[2] Practicing attorneys warn, "Try to prompt the client to have the same honesty standard . . . the smartest lawyer cannot bind two people if one is not honorable."[3]

Daniel Coquillette asks in his book on moral responsibility, "Should the negotiator believe that morality is relative, that one's notion of goodness is something entirely personal to each negotiator? Should the negotiator feel, as the Greek cynics and sophists felt, that all that is needed to assure success is rhetoric, logic and advocacy? Because there is so much difficulty in defining the nature of goodness, does that mean that it can be changed by public opinion?"[4]

The more clearly we see the reality of the world, the better able we are to deal with it. Our view of reality is like a map with which to negotiate the terrain of life. If the map is true and accurate, we will know where we are and how to get where we want to go; otherwise, we will be lost.[5]

> ***Insights from a Fresh Perspective:*** *Sacrosanct to all Albanians, from olden days to recent times, is the concept of the* besa, *or pledged word. More respected than a written contract, the verbal* besa-besën *agreement was sealed by a handshake or embrace. Woe to the person who violated it! The greatest insult in Albania is to call a man* i-pabesë, *someone who has broken his word or is without honor.*

After World War I, President Woodrow Wilson, convinced that the world needed a League of Nations, explained, "Individual morality is the sense of right or wrong of one man. The social morality must strike an average. This is where reformers make their tragic mistake. There can be no compromise in individual morality."

Resolving ethical dilemmas that have no certain answers is why the knowledge of the highest things is so desirable. When we make use of the power of self-awareness, we use dialogue with the self to attain a higher level of effectiveness. At that moment, we are living rather than being lived.[6]

> ***Insights from a Fresh Perspective:*** *Moral druthers are the foundation of ethical behavior and are based in personal faith and spirituality. Evelyn Underhill states: "My spiritual life is not something specialized and intense—a fenced off devotional path rather difficult to cultivate, and needing to be sheltered from the cold winds of the outer world. On the contrary, it is the very source of that quality and purpose, which makes my practical life worthwhile." Underhill articulates the fact that everything flows from the spiritual, which provides purpose and meaning in life. We must have that greater purpose and meaning in order to become successful in our chosen profession. The goal in life cannot be to become a successful professional, but instead, to become a successful human being, no matter what profession.*

Practical Tips

Before negotiating, review your moral map, and anticipate probable (and possible) ethical dilemmas.

CONSIDER THE PRICE

Socrates states, "Now there is no nobler inquiry, Calicles, than that which you censure me for making—what ought the character of a man to be, and what his pursuits, and how far he is to go, both in maturer years and in youth?"[7]

Since winning does have a price, what are we willing to compromise in order to win? Is it worth it? The calls in the middle are easy; those on the margin are more difficult. And we cannot let anyone else influence our calls on the margin. If we do, this margin expands and we have lost professional integrity. Once it is lost, we have lost the edge in the marketplace.[8] The historian Thucydides (circa 340 B.C.E.) reasons that since the nature of men's minds does not change any more than the nature of the human body, circumstances are bound to repeat themselves, and in the same situation, men are bound to act in the same way unless it is shown to them that such a course in other days ended disastrously.[9]

President Abraham Lincoln once said, "I am not bound to win, but I am bound to be true. I am not bound to succeed, but I am bound to live by the light that I have. I must stand with anybody that stands right, and stand with him while he is right, and part with him when he goes wrong."[10]

Remember that adopting a course of action that is contrary to our moral values is likely to act as a circuit breaker to effectiveness. The lights go off.

> ***Insights from a Fresh Perspective:*** *Simone Weil asserts, "To be rooted is perhaps the most important and least recognized need of the human soul." Our culture, inclusive of our profession, fails to recognize the need to take time to cultivate character. Instead, we forgo this fundamental need in a quest for more highly esteemed pursuits. Like a hiker who, on his way up the mountain, forgets a bottle of water in his hurry, our quest is futile from the outset without integrity.*

A school chaplain summarizes why good ethics is good business:

> First. Having a well-thought-out, tried value or ethical system gives purpose, meaning, and direction to one's life, both personal and professional. Most people cannot compartmentalize life very easily or well. Many, if not all, need a degree of inner coherence to survive, much less to thrive, emotionally and intellectually.
>
> Second. A well-grounded ethical outlook allows one to place much less reliance on external rewards as the primary motivator and validator of one's existence. If one is trapped on the endless treadmill, grasping forever greater fame, money, power, influence, whatever, one has simply degenerated into a rather pathetic puppet. Such external rewards are very transitory.

> Third. Operating out of an ethical system will not always, but often, generate a degree of trust and respect from one's peers and opponents. Trust is an elusive quality, one which emerges out of both reasoned experience and gut instinct.
>
> Fourth. Ethics are rooted in one's life within a community, or more precisely, out of the groups of communities to which one belongs. When Aristotle praised justice as the first virtue of political and civil life, he did so in such a way as to suggest that a community that lacks practical agreement on a conception of justice must also lack the necessary basis for political or civil community.[11]

Practicing a genuine ethical value system will provide the framework for success. We can find great freedom and liberation if we know the rules and are comfortable with the choices that we make. This provides the inner coherence and integrity for living our lives well. If nothing else, it makes us more relaxed and comfortable people, and this is quite an achievement.

Having Hardball Detachment

In baseball, toughness requires a balance between detachment and sensitivity. In order to be an effective leader, the hardball player needs a special kind of detachment which reflects an earnest concern for justice, maintains a perspective on the greater good, and achieves a balance between organizational goals and the broader needs of society.[12]

David Ortiz of the Boston Red Sox was asked what his thoughts were when it was his turn to bat and he stepped up to the plate with the crowd roaring. He responded, "Actually, I get more calm. In those situations, I don't want to get too excited. When you get too excited, you overexert yourself to do too much. I go through the play like I am going to have a hot tea in the morning. I quiet everything down. I try to be as quiet as I can at the plate, but still aggressive."[13]

> ***Insights from a Fresh Perspective:*** *Mark Twain once said, "It is curious—curious that physical courage should be so common in the world, and moral courage so rare." We often find ourselves faced with moral/ethical dilemmas. Such situations present the*

opportunity to exhibit moral courage, which Twain said was so lacking in the world. While it is often easier to make excuses or rationalize unethical behavior, the difficult (and eventually more rewarding) course of action involves standing up for what you believe in. We should conduct ourselves in a manner recommended by H. Jackson Brown, Jr.: "Live so that when your children think of fairness and integrity, they think of you."

Using the Five P's of Ethical Power

The Five Principles of Ethical Power are Purpose, Pride, Patience, Persistence, and Perspective.[14] Timeless values include loyalty, integrity, honor, fair play, and respect for and service to others.[15]

Integrity involves discerning right from wrong and requires that we act on what we have distinguished as right and wrong even in the face of adversity. The first criterion captures the idea that integrity requires a degree of moral reflection. The second brings in the ideal of a person of integrity as steadfast, a quality that includes keeping commitments. The third is a reminder that a person of integrity can be trusted.[16]

To get past "no," we need to understand what lies behind the "no" and overcome the barriers to cooperation: negative emotions, negotiating habits, skepticism about the benefits of agreement, perceived power, and reaction.[17] Along with the facts, there must be meaning; otherwise, the facts do not make sense. Facts need to be woven into patterned narrative in order to be remembered. It is the narrative—not the facts—that awakens the imagination.

Insights from a Fresh Perspective: *If you are loyal to your company, your family, and yourself, then you will know the right things to do. Remaining loyal during a negotiation could be the toughest thing to follow throughout the process. It's tough when you could potentially win a negotiation by telling a little fib. What do you do? You do the right thing: tell the truth and aspire to win honestly.*

Sensing ethical patterns and making moral decisions should be a shared endeavor, not something we always do alone. Instead, seek out the advice of trusted friends and colleagues. Many times we will find that the mere shaping of the question, in and of itself, points toward viable alternatives.

CONSIDER, "WHAT IS CONSCIENCE?"[18]

A Voice

The dictate of our conscience is given a privileged place when we're asked to explain why we made certain ethical decisions. But what is conscience? Is it a divine voice speaking quietly within? Is it a tool we can use to steer ourselves through crises? Is it a strong feeling that we should do something? Or is it the accumulated voices of parents and elders that have come to shape our attitudes in life?

One familiar view of conscience is found in Walt Disney's *Pinocchio,* where Jiminy Cricket assumes the role of conscience. Before Jiminy Cricket falls asleep, a fairy comes and gives the wooden toy, Pinocchio, the gift of life. "Am I a real boy?" he asks.

The fairy says no, but if Pinocchio proves himself brave, truthful, and unselfish, someday he will become a real boy. "You must learn to choose between right and wrong," the fairy tells him.

"But how will I do that?" he wonders. She tells him that he must learn to listen to his conscience. "What is conscience?," he asks.

Jiminy explains, "I'll tell you what a conscience is: conscience is the still small voice that people won't listen to."

"Are you my conscience?," Pinocchio asks Jiminy.

"Who, me?" he asks. And the fairy asks him if he would like to be Pinocchio's conscience. After he bashfully agrees, she officially makes him Pinocchio's conscience, asking him to kneel as in a knighting ceremony.

"I dub you Pinocchio's conscience, lord high keeper of the knowledge of right and wrong, counselor in moments of temptation, and guide along the straight and narrow path." At this moment she touches him with her wand and momentarily transforms his appearance with a glow.

Herein lies a classic account of what conscience is. Conscience is the knowledge of right and wrong. Conscience provides moral guidance in the face of temptation and uncertainty. What is not obvious, especially when presented in a story like *Pinocchio,* is the way in which conscience is portrayed as something outside of "us."

A Compass

Some say that conscience is more like an internal moral compass rather than an outside voice. Sometimes we are not sure what principles ought to guide us, and we may be confused about how to apply them to circumstances. So we rely upon our intuitive feeling to direct us.

An Activity

Another way to think about conscience is to think of it as an activity rather than a thing. Conscience is what we do rather than something we use or possess. Instead of a compass, conscience is better seen as the activity of consulting—of looking, thinking, reflecting, and evaluating.

USE TWO LEVELS OF ETHICAL DECISION-MAKING

Two levels exist in ethical decision-making. The first is to distinguish the clearly unethical decisions from the ethical ones. The second level involves choosing between ethical values—such as between truth and fairness or truth and loyalty—and where no single answer is absolutely right or wrong. Here, we simply have to analyze the situation as clearly as possible and be sensitive to values to consider whether we are dealing with an ethical value or a non-ethical value. It's one thing to sacrifice truth for fairness; it's another thing to sacrifice truth for success. We should only sacrifice one ethical principle for another ethical principle.[19]

Every game is composed of two parts: an outer game and an inner game. The outer game is played against an external opponent to overcome external obstacles and to reach an external goal. Neither mastery nor satisfaction can be found in playing any game without giving some attention to the relatively neglected skills of the inner game. This is the game that takes place in the mind of the player, and it is played against such obstacles as lapses in concentration, nervousness, self-doubt and self-condemnation.[20]

> ***Insights from a Fresh Perspective:*** *The smallest things that we do or say and, sometimes more importantly, what we don't do or say,*

are all seeds that we toss out on our journey. Many of these seeds may never take root, but some will. We can't control where most of the seeds fall, and we may not ever know what became of those seeds. Tiny seeds of dishonesty on our part may go forgotten after a time in our own minds, but we are powerless over when and where they will decide to grow long after we have forgotten. When our own tiny seeds of dishonesty grow in our lives and choke out what is good, it can cloud our discernment, warp our judgment, and ultimately darken our souls. Left unchecked, an innocent twisting of facts might lead to a deeper rooting of dishonesty.

Asking Questions Directed at the Process

Following the rules involves more than just knowing the difference between right and wrong. We must also acquire the wisdom and technique to find the best approach to making moral decisions. One effective approach is to ask not simply a "yes" or "no" question but a series of questions directed at the process.

Sometimes looking to the past clarifies a present dilemma. Aristotle said:

> It is by doing just acts that the just man is produced, and by doing temperate acts the temperate man; without doing these no one would have even a prospect of becoming good but most people do not do these things, but instead take refuge in theory and think they are being philosophers and will become good in this way, behaving somewhat like patients who listen attentively to their doctors, but do none of the things they are ordered to do. As the latter will not be made well in body by such a course of treatment, the former will not be made well in soul by such a course of philosophy.[21]

Distinguishing Between Ethics and Morality

Ethics is the study of what constitutes good and bad conduct. Morality is a guide to action based on the principles of compassion, truthfulness, fairness, accountability, and self-restraint created through self-awareness.[22] Harry Truman says that "most people know the difference between right and wrong; it's doing the right thing that's the hard part." In addition, Mark Twain's classic quote on the subject points to the need for a morality that is practiced publicly: "Always do right. This will gratify some people and astonish the rest."[23]

Dealing with Negotiator Misrepresentation

Negotiator misrepresentation is difficult to define because it is entwined with the subtleties of communication; it is complex to cover by laws, rules, and regulations because of the huge variety of substantive situations involved. Tort law provides liability for fraudulent representation.[24] Contract law provides that a contract is rendered void if based upon a fraudulent or a material misrepresentation.[25] Agency law provides that an agent making fraudulent misrepresentations can be held personally liable. There are unfair trade practices in security transactions, CPA regulations, lawyer's rules of professional conduct, and other applicable regulations governing misrepresentation.

Practical Tips

Like the poker player, Mr. Negotiator wants the opponent to overestimate the value of his hand. He must facilitate the opponent's inaccurate assessment. Deception is at the core of many negotiation tactics and strategies. A certain amount of "embellishment" and withholding of your reservation price is expected. So—how do you negotiate ethically? How do you bluff about the bottom line and still be truthful?

- "Is this your best price?"
- "At this time my best price is__________"
- "What is your bottom line assessment?"
- "My present assessment of the value is__________"

The best approach, the right approach, and smart approach is simply to avoid, at all costs, making any false factual statement such as, "I am not authorized to go below $50,000" (when the authority is actually $40,000); instead, use a non-deceptive alternative such as, "In my opinion, this case is worth at least $50,000, and I'm not going to recommend a lower figure at this time (you follow with an explanation justifying your opinion)." Another approach is to ask the principal or client to give only the authority you want at the time.

Sometimes, it is more appropriate simply to deflect the authority question by saying, "Joe, you know we can't discuss authority, either one of us, so let's talk about what is fair." But remember that the consideration of possible interpretations of ethical rules is never complete without referring back to what you stand for as an individual.

American Bar Association Model Rules of Professional Conduct

Ethical rules for lawyers contain much wisdom that can serve as a helpful guide to other negotiators.

- MR 2.1 provides: "In representing a client, a lawyer shall exercise independent professional judgment and render candid advice. In rendering advice, a lawyer may refer not only to law, but to other considerations such as moral, economic, social and political factors that may be relevant to the client's situation."[26]
- MR 4.1 states: Do not knowingly "make a false statement of material fact or law."[27] Official comment: "This Rule refers to statements of fact. Whether a particular statement should be regarded as one of fact can depend on the circumstances. Under generally accepted conventions in negotiations, certain types of statements ordinarily are not taken as statements of material fact. Estimates of price or value placed on the subject of a transaction and a party's intention as to an acceptable settlement of a claim are in this category, and so is the existence of undisclosed principal except where nondisclosure of this principal would constitute fraud."[28]
- MR 8.4 provides: "It is professional misconduct for a lawyer to . . . engage in conduct involving dishonesty, fraud, deceit, or misrepresentation."[29] The official comment to this Rule provides: "As negotiator, a lawyer seeks a result advantageous to the client but consistent with requirements of honest dealing with others. . . . Many of a lawyer's professional

responsibilities are prescribed in the Rules of Professional Conduct, as well as substantive and procedural law. However, a lawyer is also guided by personal conscience and the approbation of professional peers. A lawyer should strive to attain the highest level of skill, to improve the law and the legal profession, and to exemplify the legal profession's ideals of public service."[30]

Practical Tips

The best practical advice on exercising good judgment involving ethics is to anticipate what situation is likely to come up and what type of moral dilemmas are likely to be presented. This advance planning not only simplifies the decisions but also reduces the necessity of making quick, on-the-spot calls in the heat of battle. Judgment decisions are often rendered more difficult because of a neglect to anticipate and prepare for what was clearly on the horizon.[31]

To stimulate this anticipation, consider asking yourself the following questions:

- Is there an affirmative duty to inform the other of relevant facts? Of material facts? Hidden assets?
- What is my duty to inform the other of the other's drafting error? To correct the other's erroneous factual or legal assumptions? Which representations are of fact? Of opinion? What constitutes mere puffing?
- How can I ethically avoid disclosing certain information? How do I deal with nibbling? How can I best partially disclose pertinent information? Once I start, is complete disclosure required?

Thinking About Lying

Lying requires a reason while truth-telling does not. Liars usually weigh only the immediate harm to others from the lie against the benefits desired. The flaw in this is that it underestimates two additional kinds of harm—the harm that lying does to the liars and the harm done to the general level of trust and social cooperation. Both are cumulative and hard to reverse. Trust and integrity are precious resources that are easily squandered and hard to regain. They can thrive only on a foundation of respect for veracity.[32]

> ***Insights from a Fresh Perspective:*** *I come to a single word as my leading lesson learned in negotiations: balance. I say this because each of the skills and techniques learned seem to point to a balance in negotiation. This doesn't simply mean that a good negotiator splits everything down the middle 50/50. Rather, he looks deeper into the situation to find the true balance of the negotiation. This proved to be a hard lesson for many of us to learn, as engineers tend to look at every issue from a numbers-based perspective. In accordance with the cover design of this book, we must balance our "competitive" skills with the timeless values that we all hold. It is only with an appropriate balance of these two factors can we negotiate effectively.*

Increasing Confidence and Becoming More Skilled

Our confidence as negotiators has increased and will continue to do so because of insights gained in Part I: knowing what we stand for as individuals and what we have to offer of value before we start to negotiate; how to recognize the patterns; and how to follow the rules.

It is time for us to become more skilled as negotiators through active listening, well-planned strategies, focused tactics, and the use of the mediation open-ended question.

Look for an ethical pattern developing.

Summary

- Review your moral maps before starting a negotiation, and use them as a guide.
- Accept the principle that good ethics is good business.
- Practice anticipating and resolving morally complex issues.
- Share moral decision-making.
- Avoid unethical misrepresentation.

NOTES

1. Geoffrey C. Hazard, Jr. and Angelo Dondi, *Legal Ethics: A Comparative Study* (Palo Alto, CA: Stanford University Press, 2004), 7.
2. Professor Howard W. L'Enfant, Louisiana State University, College of Law speaking to the class.
3. Ashton R. Hardy, attorney, New Orleans, speaking to the class.
4. Daniel R. Coquillette, *Lawyers and Fundamental Moral Responsibility: Materials,* 2nd Ed (Cincinnati, OH: Anderson Publishing Company; 1995), chapter 1.
5. M. Scott Peck, *The Road Less Traveled: A New Psychology of Love, Traditional Values and Spiritual Growth* (Touchstone, 2003), 44.
6. This paragraph was adopted from Todd L. Eckerson in "Worldviews & Decisions," a course he teaches in Ethical Philosophy at Westminster School, Simsbury, Connecticut.
7. Benjamin Jowett, *Socrates in Gorgias by Plato* (PSU Press, 1999), 107.
8. E. Graham Thompson, former President and CEO, City National Bank of Baton Rouge, speaking to the class.
9. Edith Hamilton, *The Greek Way* (New York: W.W. Norton & Company, 1993), 165.
10. Abraham Lincoln, *Quotations Book,* http://quotationsbook.com/quote/39898 (accessed, October 28, 2010).
11. The Rev. Dr. James E. Hamner, Professor-Adjunct, LSU Department of Philosophy, Assistant Headmaster and Chaplain, Episcopal High School, Baton Rouge, speaking to the class (emphasis added).
12. Jeffrey A. Banach "The Ethics of Hardball" *California Management Review,* 1985 27.2. 132–39. Adopted from a course taught by Jeffrey A. Barach, Professor of Management, A. B. Freeman School of Business, Tulane University.
13. David Ortiz, *Time* 169.23 (June 4, 2007), under "10 Questions for David Ortiz," http://www.time.com/time/magazine/article/0,9171,1625198,00.html

14. Kenneth Blanchard and Norman Vincent Peale, *The Power of Ethical Management* (New York: William Morrow and Company, 1988), 79.
15. James P. McCallie, President, Darlington School, Rome, Georgia.
16. Stephen L. Carter, "The Insufficiency of Honesty," in Atlantic Monthly (February 1996), 74–76.
17. William Ury, *Getting Past No, Negotiating With Difficult People,* Rev. Ed. (New York: Bantam Books, 1993), 79.
18. This section adopted from the Reverend Stephen Holmgren, *Ethics After Easter* (Cambridge, MA: Cowley Publications, 2000), 119–123.
19. Adopted from Todd L. Eckerson in his class on Worldviews & Decisions.
20. W. Timothy Gallwey, *The Inner Game of Tennis,* (New York: Random House, 1997), introduction.
21. Aristotle, *The Nicomachean Ethics.* (Oxford World's Classics, 1998), 35.
22. Todd L. Eckerson, from lecture entitled "Teaching Ethics."
23. John Bartlett, *Familiar Quotations,* (Emily Morison Beck ed., 14th ed., 1968), 763. Mark Twain was writing to Greenpoint Presbyterian Church, Brooklyn, New York, Feb. 16, 1901.
24. Restatement of Torts § 525.
25. Restatement of Contracts § 164.
26. The ABA Model Rules of Professional Conduct, Model Rules 2.1.
27. The ABA Model Rules of Professional Conduct, Model Rules 4.1 [a].
28. The ABA Model Rules of Professional Conduct, Comment to Rule 4.1.
29. The ABA Model Rules of Professional Conduct, Model Rules 8.4 [c].
30. The ABA Model Rules of Professional Conduct, Preamble, adopted by the ABA House of Delegates, amended 2002.
31. James C. Fruend, an attorney with the firm of Skadden, Arps, Slate, Meagher & Flom LLP, New York City, and the author of *Lawyering: A Realistic Approach to Legal Practice*

(Law Journal Seminars-Press, 1979), and, "A Time to Reap" *Business Law Journal* November/December 1997, 13–18.

32. Sissela Bok, *Lying: Moral Choice in Public and Private Life* (New York, Random House/Vintage, 1999), 24, 52–55. Bok is Instructor in Ethics in Harvard Medical School.

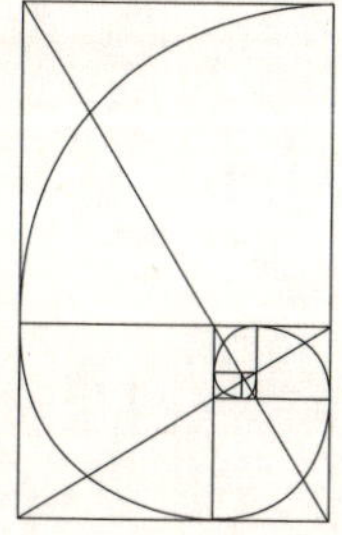

Part II:

Becoming More Skilled

Component Four:

Listen with Four Ears

Honing This Skill to Repeat under Pressure

A lack of focused listening with all of your senses has the power to derail each and every negotiating skill, including the best strategies, the sharpest tactics, and the most honed mediation techniques. What a sobering thought! Just think of how much is missed by not actively listening to what others are saying.

What a negotiator often encounters is not a problem to be solved but an idea to be heard, a different view to be understood, or a person to get to know. Negotiating involves an encounter with the unexpected and the elements of suspense and surprise. It requires an active listening process that can only be followed and not forced. When listening, a negotiator must wait patiently for insight to emerge and trust in the outcome of the process.[1]

In golf, we practice in order to find a golf swing that will repeat under pressure.[2] Just as practicing our swing helps with golf, what method is most meaningful in dealing with people and improves with use? The most important negotiation skill to practice—call it our golf swing—is learning to listen very carefully. The keys to improving this skill are alertness, awareness, relaxed concentration, and the ability to focus and observe.

When we try to do too many things at once, it is impossible to be present-moment oriented. Few individuals are good conversationalists because many think of what they intend to say rather than about what the other is saying.[3]

Therefore, our focus in this component "is not just to hear but to listen."[4] Many people believe that if we can hear, we can listen—and that's as ridiculous as believing that if we can see, we can read. *Hearing* is mostly physical; *listening* is mostly psychological. When asked which she would prefer, the restoration of her hearing or her sight, Helen Keller replied, "Hearing." This decision continues to be born out by the many examples of people who, after losing their sight, become acute listeners.

Our approach to improving our listening is in four parts, one for each of the four ears of listening:

- **First ear**—Listen to what is clearly being said.
- **Second ear**—Listen to what is clearly not being said.
- **Third ear**—Listen for what the other is attempting to say but isn't.
- **Fourth ear**—Listen to what we are saying to ourselves.

FIRST EAR: LISTEN TO WHAT IS CLEARLY BEING SAID

Our first ear of listening involves listening actively (participating and concentrating) to gain insight into the thoughts, needs, and feelings of others. My wife wisely points out, "By listening actively and not mentally preparing your immediate reply, you are less likely to convey unintended nonverbal signals."[5] Remember that we hear only the sounds to which we listen.[6] Peter, Paul, and Mary said it another way: "How many ears does a man have to have to hear someone crying?"[7]

> ***Insights from a Fresh Perspective:*** *"A Love Supreme," "Transition," "First Meditations," "Om," and "Meditations" are magnificent albums by John Coltrane. Coltrane incorporates elements of Indian music, such as repetition droning to create interactions with the audience. In a negotiation, an opponent wants to feel that you're creating something with or through them. If they feel you came to hear yourself play, you have lost not only your own sound but the voice of those who came to hear you.*

Active listening, involves catching the meaning sent. This is analogous to catching a baseball. Can you imagine the catcher not being actively involved? Catching the ball is just as much an activity as pitching it, sending it on its way. The art of catching is the art of catching every kind of pitch—fastballs, curves, change-ups, and knuckleballs. But the analogy to listening is flawed because in baseball, the ball is a simple unit. It is completely caught or not. A spoken message, however, is a complex object. It can be received completely or in a way unlike what the speaker intended. The amount the listener catches depends on the listening skills of the listener.

Uncovering Feelings and Motives

Special Agent Edgar M. Wines once commented that people primarily want interviewers to understand their ideas, emotions, and attitudes. Facts alone are used only to support these ideas. This means that the negotiator should read the other person with eyes that hear and with ears that see in order to reconstruct not just the facts but the ideas. Betty Edwards, in her writing on artistic success, states that there is more to seeing than meets the eyeball.[8] Think of every thought, feeling, and movement as having its own musical qualities and the ear as a regulated instrument that can be fine tuned.[9]

Practical Tip

A good way to listen is to reconstruct the ideas of the person speaking. Use the other's facts for constructing the idea. Remembering the idea will help you retain the facts far better than just trying to remember the facts by themselves.

Feelings and motives are so important in listening to what is being said that when they are removed by electronic communication, much of what otherwise would be clearly said is lost. In addition, it is sometimes the very smallest of subtleties, repeated over and over, which form a predictable pattern and send a clear message.[10]

Listening Between the Words

Listen between the words to hear more than just the words, to hear a particular message. Try the Greek approach of focusing first on *ethos* (culture, background, disposition, character); second on *pathos* (feelings, emotions); and only later on *logos* (philosophy, reason).

> ***Insights from a Fresh Perspective:*** *As the conductor takes his stand, it is essential that every member of a two-hundred-piece orchestra understands the conductors' signals. As the conductor, he must direct by using visual signals because he can't audibly tell the members of the orchestra what to do; they must watch for the signals, know, and understand. The same rule applies for negotiations. When first entering the room, the negotiator must set the tone.*

Note that some people do not talk in order to formulate their ideas but to vent their feelings. Understand that these same people often go on repeating the same thing until their emotive discharge is complete. When we realize the distinction between these two forms of speech, we will discover that this is the key to many of life's mistakes. When the other person speaks in order to express an idea, discussion is legitimate—not to discuss the idea put forward would be not to take the other person seriously. Such discussion is fruitful and throws new light on the subject. But when the other speaks in order to vent feelings, it is necessary to listen without discussion. In this case, discussion leads to misapprehensions and gives the feeling that the other person is not being understood.[11]

People are not computers programmed to respond to impulses from the other side. Human beings have feelings generated by the negotiation process—feelings of mistrust, fear, and anger. Active listening is a process of thoroughly hearing what the other has said and responding with a reflective statement that mirrors what has been heard.[12] The focus here is the ability to see the situation as the other side does. We should understand empathetically the power of the other's point of view and feel the emotional force with which the other believes in it.[13]

Listening between the words is what the little prince does when he comes across a fox he would like to get to know. He asks the fox, "What must I do to tame a fox?"

The fox says, "You must come to this spot in the woods several days at the same time and just wait because we only understand the thing we tame."

"But what must I do to tame you?"

"Sit there a while, look, don't talk . . . be very patient. You will say nothing. Words are a source of misunderstanding."[14]

> ***Insights from a Fresh Perspective:*** *Listening is not just an action; it is an active process. Many people confuse "hearing" with "listening." In order to be a good listener, you must involve much more than just your ears. When working as a coach of the football team, I used a technique called "SLANT," which stands for Sit up, Listen, Act interested, Nod your head, and Track the person speaking. Understanding what someone is trying to say involves all of your senses. In most cases, it is what the person doesn't say that carries more weight than the actual words being said. I am a firm believer that you can read anyone and the message that they are trying to get across by "listening with your eyes."*

Listening to Facial Expressions and Voice Tone

In Leo Tolstoy's *War and Peace*, we are told to visualize a military general sitting on a bench, his gray head hanging, his heavy body relaxed. The general listens to the reports that are brought to him and gives directions when his subordinates demand it of him; but when listening to the reports, it seems that he is not interested in the import of the words spoken; instead, the general focuses on the facial expression and tone of voice of those who are reporting. Through long years of military experience and the wisdom of age, he knows and understands that it is impossible for one man to direct hundreds of thousands of others struggling with death. He knows that the result of a battle is decided not by the orders of a commander-in-chief, by the place where the troops are stationed, nor by the number of cannons or slaughtered men, but by that intangible force called the spirit of the army: he watches this force and guides it to the best of his ability.[15]

Listening through the Pause

As we listen through the pause, we gain additional insight. Often during this pause, non-verbal signals from the other provide an indication of what the other is planning to say but is hesitant to express in words.

Practical Tip

Confirm what you think you've heard by replying, "So, what you are saying is . . . "

SECOND EAR: LISTEN FOR WHAT OBVIOUSLY IS NOT BEING SAID

Our second ear of listening involves recognizing what speech conceals and what silence reveals.[16] Listen for and observe carefully how the other person listens to and interprets what we are saying. Napoleon, the tactician of many military campaigns, asserted that we should never interrupt an opponent because he may be in the process of making a mistake.

I remember learning my lesson on this subject from listening to my children. My wife and our four small children, all under the age of ten, were returning along a rocky creek bank from swimming. I overheard my oldest son, Hutch, ask his mother, "Why are some of these rocks green?" She said, "Ask your Dad." Then he said something barely audible to his mother: "Mom, I don't want to know that much."

Recognizing Why Gender Matters

Hearing what is not being said by the other involves listening with our eyes and other senses. These other senses are not the same for everyone.

Deborah Tannen, in her book about gender roles in communication, *You Just Don't Understand: Women and Men in Conversation,* describes why gender matters, particularly in conversation and listening. She points out that men and women should learn from each other, the best from each. Females typically have a greater capacity to listen patiently to all of the nuances in conversation. Males, on the other hand, tend to be more focused on the core meaning of the message. Every person has a touch of both. Each person should try to utilize both the male and female aspects of his or her character.[17]

Leonard Sax, M.D., Ph.D. (Harvard), reveals in his book *Why Gender Matters* that innate differences in hearing and seeing exist between male and female. The hemispheric compartmentalization of function obvious in a man's brain (left brain verbal, right brain spatial) "applies less well or not at all to female brains." Female brain tissue is "intrinsically different" from male brain tissue. Furthermore, it is shown that not only is information and emotion processed differently, but the female actually hears better because female hearing is "substantially more sensitive—especially in the 1,000 to 4,000 Hz range, which is so important in speech discrimination." One example given is that of a forty-three-year-old man talking to his seventeen-year-old daughter. He thinks he is talking in a normal tone, but she feels he is "yelling at her." This is because she is going to "experience his voice as being about ten times louder than what the man is hearing." The man experiences an even more pronounced difference when he is trying to listen to a soft female voice. He can't hear her. Similar differences exist in seeing because the retina is constructed and connected to the brain differently. The female is able to "make more elaborate and more subtle color distinctions" and to read facial expressions better.[18]

Practical Tips

Look not only for the reaction that the other has to what you have just said but also for what the other obviously is not saying out loud. In addition, look for words and signs pointing to the opposite of what is being said, as when the other prefaces with "frankly," or, "to tell you the truth . . . "

Help the other to listen—package conclusions by giving reasons first and proposals second (if the reverse is done, they will be busy thinking about their response and may not hear one word of explanation).

A big mistake in negotiating is reasoning with someone who is angry. Instead, acknowledge feelings first and allow emotional dialogue to precede intellectual discussion.

Ask these questions:

- What is my opponent's frame of reference?
- What situation does this opponent find him/herself in?
- What does this opponent consider to be essential in this situation?
- What emotions should be encouraged or discouraged?

Polish your listening skills with these tactics:

- Listen full time. Tuning out for even five seconds can cause you to fall behind.
- Address questions directly. Never respond to direct questions by babbling or telling long anecdotes.
- Acknowledge what you hear. If you can't give a quick answer, at least explain why. Example: "To answer that, I should give you some background first."
- Go with the flow. If the conversation changes direction, go with it. Don't look for the first opportunity to get back to your favorite subject, or you won't hear what the other person is saying.

Keeping Their Wavelength in Mind

To effectively listen to another, we should step to the other person's side, use small talk to warm up, and use the other's wavelength by tuning into the other's communicative manner (fast/slow, loud/soft). Try to communicate through those senses (seeing, listening, feeling, touching, reasoning) to which the other is more apt to respond.[19]

> ***Insights from a Fresh Perspective:*** *In China, I took some piano lessons when I was young. I didn't grow up to be a great musician like my parents had hoped for; however, these lessons helped me develop a deep understanding of music. My piano teacher used to tell me over and over again:* "Xuan wai zhi yin . . ." *The direct translation is: "To listen to what is behind the music . . ." He showed me that the only way to understand music was to "see" the picture behind the notes, to "hear" the whisper beyond the sound. That is where the conductor's deep emotions and feelings lie. We have been told to listen "with eyes that hear and with ears that see." We need to listen beyond the words to understand where our opponents are coming from.*

Expecting the Unexpected

Listening involves ambiguity and waiting for the unexpected. Negotiators are required not only to grasp an idea but also to simultaneously get to know a person. Hearing clearly what is not being said sometimes involves a paradox of not trying too hard.

Since moving to the mountains of North Carolina, the biggest problem I have had with developing a solid golf swing (and perhaps in becoming a better listener) involves gripping the golf club too tightly and trying too hard. The best control is achieved not by grabbing the club with all the strength of both hands but by holding it loosely with confidence that the club head will reach its maximum speed and interface with the ball correctly. In order to hold the club more effectively, I must let go a little; in order to exercise the greatest control, I need to relax; in order to practice my swing to repeat under pressure, I must reduce the pressure in both arms and hands.

In archery, sometimes the shot will go smoothly only when it takes the archer himself by surprise.[20] The swing of the golf club with the "lightest" of hands (with just enough pressure to keep the club from slipping) creates maximum power and consistency. This swing can be accomplished by those who are confident, relaxed, sure of their position, sure of the shot required, and sure of their ability to make it. Just as understanding this concept improves a golf swing, so will it improve a negotiator's ability to listen effectively.

THIRD EAR: LISTEN FOR WHAT THE OTHER REALLY WANTS TO SAY, BUT DOESN'T

Our third ear of listening involves listening for the logos, the essence of things.[21] For example, in a family law matter, we must learn to listen to what the clients are trying to tell us.[22] A useful reminder is to use the "e" and "a" and "r" of "ear": Explore what is not clear, acknowledge what is understood, and then respond.[23]

Practical Tips

Examples of communication senses are:

- "I see what you are saying" (eyes)
- "You have a point there" (reason)
- "I hear you" (ears)
- "I know exactly what you mean" (reason)
- "I would feel the same way too" (feelings)
- "I'm comfortable with that" (feelings)

- "The way I see it . . ." (eyes)

Use your opponent's name as you make eye contact.

Focus on issues on which you already agree (this builds momentum).

Use the word "yes" (followed by "and" not "but") for unity, not dichotomy of thought, and speak only for yourself. This will acknowledge the person, his or her authority, and his or her competence:

- "Yes, you have a point there, and . . ."
- "Yes, I agree with you, and . . ."

Hearing What Is Really Meant

Particularly in crisis negotiations, we must use active listening. This requires expertise in discussing and conferring with, as opposed to bargaining against, in order to hear what the other person is really saying. We must listen to understand rather than attempt to achieve an agreement or produce some kind of change in the other person.[24]

> ***Insights from a Fresh Perspective:*** *When people speak in China, especially in a negotiation, they rethink the things they are saying at the same time; therefore, they will insert longer or shorter pauses during speaking to give themselves time to think and get feedback from the opponent. If we can catch these pauses, we can get a better idea of what other people are planning to do but hesitate to express. Go ahead, offer your understanding to encourage them to express what they hesitate to say. By doing this, you are at least benefiting from the following two prospects: 1) Logically, you can get a better insight to what your opponents are expressing; 2) Emotionally, you post a friendly gesture even before the intellectual analysis begins, which usually leads to an agreeable discussion.*

Don't just hear the words of the other person, seek to understand what that person really means. What a person says is an imperfect representation of what that person is thinking or trying to say. So we listen to what the other person says and then make inferences about what that person is thinking in order to penetrate the thoughts behind the words. Communications in negotiations need to cover all important concerns, reveal all parties' issues and interests, and explore likely avenues of mutual gain. Sometimes it is helpful to use a metaphor to describe an indirect meaning.[25]

Take, for example, the Universal Translator from the television series *Star Trek*. Whenever the U.S.S. *Enterprise* encounters an unknown alien from some distant quadrant of the universe, the stranger's voice is heard in perfect, colloquial English. The alien language is translated instantaneously by this device. Likewise, we must skillfully translate what is being said into what the speaker intends to say.[26]

> ***Insights from a Fresh Perspective:*** *The Chinese have a character phrase,* 洗耳恭听, *which means "listening with respectful attention." The first character means "wash," the second means "ear." In ancient Chinese, "washing the ear and then listening" can be a respectful way of listening to others. The third character means "respectful." The upperside of this character means "concentrated" or "together." It has an indication that if we "concentrate our mind all together to do something it will show respect to that speaking person." The left part of the last character, "listen," means "mouth," where the "sounds" come from.*

Being Receptive to the Thoughts of the Other

Real listening involves being receptive to the thoughts, ideas, and emotions of the other, particularly those which are not specifically expressed. We must open the lines of communication and relax. Clients may hire us to talk, but first, as professionals, we must listen and listen well.[27]

The actor Peter Sellers, in his role as Inspector Clouseau, approaches the check-in counter in an English country hotel. In front of him is a small man with a large dog. Sellers asks, "Does your dog bite?" The man replies, "No, sihr." Sellers does not hear what the man left out. As he approaches the counter, he is promptly bitten by the dog and exclaims, "I thought you said your dog doesn't bite!" The man replies, "Zaht ees noht my dogg!"

To listen well with the third ear, the mind of the listener must be open, non-judgmental, and actively concentrated on understanding the other's message. One of the primary tasks of the listener is to stay out of the speaker's way so the listener can discover how the speaker views the situation. This concept is summarized well by Edward G. Bulwer-Lytton, "The true spirit of conversation consists in building on another man's observation, not overturning it."[28]

FOURTH EAR: LISTEN TO WHAT YOU ARE SAYING TO YOURSELF

Our fourth ear of listening involves perhaps the most important part of listening—listening to our perceptions and the voices from within. Talking to ourselves may result in the discovery that our informed intuition, our inner coach, is often the best and wisest conversation partner we will ever have.

Practical Tips

After others stop talking, remember that they may not mean exactly what they just said. Wait a moment before speaking. They may want to add something.

Listening with Our Informed Intuition

We are constantly training our informed intuition so that it is ready, willing, and able to help us listen, discern, and decide. It supplies an immediate, instinctive reaction about which we do not have to consciously think.

Asking questions results in opening an inner space to receive the reply.[29] I have found it helpful to visualize the space created to process the reply as being similar to the scientific concept of space-time as a large web-like mat. Any large celestial body (a strong preconceived thought or feeling about the subject) exerts such a strong gravitational force that the mat (the space created to process a reply) is greatly warped.[30] For example, we may have experienced such an adverse reaction to what the other has just said that we are incapable of picking up on the hidden messages from the other.

When listening, we should use our antennae of perception—our mind, memory, will, emotions, and imagination.[31] It has been pointed out that the best thoughts always come from others[32] and that when the mind talks, the body should listen.[33]

A keen observer who finds himself steadily repelled by some apparently trifling thing in negotiations is right to give it great weight. It may be the clue to the whole mystery. Remember, a hair or two will show where a lion is hidden; a very little key will open a very heavy door.[34]

> ***Insights from a Fresh Perspective:*** *We really don't know why we make some decisions, especially those that come to us suddenly. We want to try to make sense of the world, including that which depends on the subconscious. We think we know, but we don't. For example, look at a baseball pitcher and the batter at home plate. The batter does not know what the pitcher is going to throw, but he has to rely on his gut to determine if he should swing or not. What we know of our motivations and choices is incomplete. If we are to learn to improve the quality of the decisions we make, we need to accept the mysterious nature of our snap judgments. We need to respect the fact that it is possible to know without knowing why we know and simply accept that fact.*

Looking For Ideas to Prove Us Wrong

People spend most of their waking hours communicating. But consider this: while the majority of society spends years learning how to read, write, and speak, how much time is spent learning how to listen? What training or education has enabled men and women to listen so that they truly understand one another without misinterpretation. "Seek first to understand" involves a very deep shift in paradigm. One typically seeks first to be understood. Scholars point out that many people do not listen with the intent to understand; they listen with the intent to reply. They are either speaking or preparing to speak. They are filtering everything through their own paradigms; they are reading their autobiography into other people's lives. "Oh, I know exactly how you feel!" "I went through the very same thing. Let me tell you about my experience." They are constantly projecting their own home movies onto other people's behavior. They prescribe their own glasses for everyone with whom they interact.[35]

Emotion can act as a filter as it hunts for evidence to prove an opponent wrong and prove us right. To counter this tendency, we should instead hunt for ideas that might prove our own assumptions wrong (as well as those that may prove them right), and experiment helping an opponent really listen to what we are saying.

Avoiding the Eighteen-Second Interruption

Jerome Groopman, M.D., (a practicing physician, researcher on cancer and AIDS, and a professor at Harvard Medical School), writes about the critical mistake many doctors make when speaking with patients: "We want to be listened to, and in a high-tech age, the key to accurate diagnosis and the best insightful thinking comes from listening and language. The errors that we make in our thinking often come about because we cut off the dialogue. Most physicians interrupt a patient eighteen seconds after they start talking."[36]

Listening without Sending Unintended Signals

Have you ever noticed the facial expressions of a television interviewer? As the answer is being given, the cameraman interrupts the close-up coverage of the one answering the question and zooms in on the face of the one who just asked the question—the one who is listening. The professional television interviewer (the listener) rarely sends any signals except those that are neutral or positive. What about those who haven't practiced this form of listening? Sometimes, while listening, people send strong unintended signals—signals that overpower the meaning of what they have just said.

This issue was illustrated in the 2000 presidential television debates between Al Gore and George W. Bush. In his book *The Assault on Reason,* Al Gore explains the effect of the overriding power of his sigh while Bush was speaking:

> As a college student, I wrote my senior thesis on the impact of television on the balance of power among the three branches of government. In the study, I pointed out the growing importance of visual rhetoric and body language over logic and reason. There are countless examples of this, but perhaps understandably, the first one that comes to mind is from the 2000 campaign, long before the Supreme Court decision and the hanging chads, when the

> controversy over my sighs in the first debate with George W. Bush created an impression on television that for many viewers outweighed whatever positive benefits I might have otherwise gained in the verbal combat of ideas and substance. A lot of good that senior thesis did me.[37]

Listening to How We Are Thinking

Albert Einstein's theory of special relativity is one hundred years old. It deals with the speed of light being consistent in all frames of reference. Einstein accomplishes this discovery without computers and other modern scientific aids; it is simply conceived in his intellect. The most important question for him was, "What, precisely, is thinking?"[38]

Sometimes it is more appropriate to use our informed intuition not to explain\, but simply to point the way.[39] The sense of smell is to an animal what intuition is to the human spirit—it tells us of the invisible, of what cannot be detected by other means, of the things that are not there, yet are coming. Intuition helps us see into the blind opaque past and round the corner of time.[40] It appears to be the extrasensory perception of reality.[41]

Often we do not arrive at conclusions by the process of quiet, logical deduction, nor yet by the blinding flash of glorious intuition, but by the untidy process halfway between the two by which we usually get to know things.[42]

Communicating in a Crisis

Communicating in a crisis with an air traffic controller while flying an airplane brings sharply into focus the two key roles of effective communication: the speaker and the listener. Nowhere is this more drastically demonstrated than in the "black box" recordings of the communications immediately preceding a tragic crash of a commercial airliner. In these last few seconds, there is not enough time to clarify the miscommunications between participants, particularly when they are from drastically different communicating cultures. The participant from a Western culture knows it is the speaker who bears full responsibility to express ideas clearly. If the other is from an Asian culture it is the listener, not the speaker, who is at fault when there is confusion. Furthermore, in Western cultures, speaking clearly requires a direct, forceful approach even when talking to a superior. Not so in Asian cultures, where speaking to a superior requires an indirect approach, never a direct approach, even in times of crisis.[43]

Listening as Part of Strategy

Good listening not only creates relationships, which help the other person listen more intently to us, but it also allows us to gather more information before we speak. We learn to take responsibility not only for how we listen but also for how we communicate. We become more aware of cultural differences in the way people communicate. We are able to detect unspoken feelings and interests that are hidden behind the façade of stated positions. Actively using all four ears to listen to all that is being communicated is a powerful strategy always to be combined with other strategies, as we will consider in our next component.

Look for a developing pattern in your listening.

Summary

- Listen intently when another is speaking, to uncover what the other is trying to say or what the other really means.
- Be receptive to the thoughts, ideas, and emotions of the one speaking.
- Use the other's "wave length" and follow your honed instincts to interpret.
- When listening, look for ideas that might prove your preconceived notions and ideas wrong.
- Allow an expression of emotion to come before starting to intellectually analyze the situation.
- Avoid sending unintentional signals while listening to another speak.

NOTES

1. Parker J. Palmer, *The Active Life: A Spirituality of Work, Creativity, and Caring* (Jossey-Bass, 1999), 74. See also, Gerry Spence, *How to Argue and Win Every Time* (New York, St. Martins, 1995) Chapter 5, "The Power of Listening."
2. Ben Hogan, *Gold Swing Control,* http://www.golfswingcontrol.com/Hoganssecret.html
3. François La Rochefoucauld, *The Quotations Page,* http://www.quotationspage.com/quote/29463.html
4. Hewlett-Packard 1997 Annual Report.
5. Eugenia Slaughter McClendon, commenting on this section.
6. "Listening is the ability to hear what people are saying or not saying as distinguished from the words they enunciate." Gerry Spence, *How to Argue and Win Every Time* (New York, St. Martins, 1995), 67.
7. From the song, "Blowing in the Wind," by Peter, Paul & Mary.
8. Chapter heading in Betty Edwards, *Drawing on the Artist Within* (Fireside, 1987), Chapter 16.
9. Don Campbell, Director of the Institute for Music, Health and Education in Boulder, Colorado.
10. Malcolm Gladwell, *The Tipping Point: How Little Things Can Make a Big Difference* (Boston: Little, Brown and Company, 2000), 74–80.
11. Paul Tournier, *The Strong and The Weak,* translated by Edwin Hudson (Louisville, KY: Westminster John Knox Press, 1976), 127.
12. Donald G. Gifford, *Gifford's Legal Negotiation Theory and Applications* (New York: West Publishing, 2001), 90.
13. Alan Scott Rau, Edward F. Sherman, and Scott. R. Peppet, *Negotiation* (Foundation Press, 2002), 126, 186, 187.
14. Antoine de Saint-Exupéry, *The Little Prince* (Harvest Books, 2000), 66–68.
15. Leo Tolstoy, *War and Peace* (New York: Random House Inc., 2004), 918.
16. Robert A. Jenks, Mediation Arbitration Professional

Systems, New Orleans, speaking to the class.

17. Deborah Tannen, *You Just Don't Understand: Women and Men in Conversation* (New York: HarperCollins, 2001), 142.
18. Leonard Sax, *Why Gender Matters: What Parents and Teachers Need to Know about the Emerging Science of Sex Differences* (Broadway, 2006), 17–18, 20.
19. Professor William Ury, speaking at the Harvard Program on Negotiation.
20. Eugen Herrigel, *Zen in the Art of Archery* (Vintage, 1999), VII, 5, 27, 48, 53.
21. Richard G. Geldard, *Remembering Heraclitus,* (New York, Steiner Books, Inc, 2000), 37.
22. Thomas K. Kirkpatrick, attorney, Baton Rouge, speaking to the class.
23. Adopted from Kenneth H. Blanchard and Spencer Johnson, *One Minute Manager,* 2nd Ed. (New York: HarperCollins Business, 2000), 17.
24. Terry Royce, in *Negotiation Journal,* January 2005, 9, 10.
25. Thomas H. Smith, in *Negotiation Journal,* July 2005, 314.
26. Mark A. Sargent, "What Does It Take? Hallmarks of the Business Lawyer," in *Business Law Today* (July/August, 1996), 11–14.
27. Milton W. Zwicker, "What Clients Really Want from their Lawyers," in *Law Practice Management* (September 1994), 24.
28. Edward Bulwer Lytton, *The Duchess de la Vallière: A Play in Five Acts* (A. W. Galignani1, 1837), 156.
29. Parker J. Palmer, *The Courage to Teach: Exploring the Inner Landscape of a Teacher's Life* (San Francisco, CA: Jossey-Bass, Inc., 1998), 46, 159.
30. Stephen W. Hawking, *The Universe in a Nutshell* (Bantam, 2001), 25.
31. John Powell, *He Touched Me* (Allen, TX: Argus Communications, 1974), 74–80.
32. Cited from"Quotation and Originality" in Emerson, Ralph Waldo. *Complete Works: Volume* 6. (Boston: Houghton Mifflin, 1904), 327.

33. Deborah Tannen. *You Just Don't Understand: Women and Men in Conversation* (New York: HarperCollins, 2001), 123–48.
34. Charles Dickens. Hunted Down. *The Oxford Book of Victorian Detective Stories.* Ed. Michael Cox. (New York: Oxford U Press, 2003), 48–68.
35. Stephen R. Covey, *Seven Habits of Highly Effective People: Powerful Lessons in Personal Change* (Free Press, 1989), 239.
36. Nancy Shute, "How Doctors Think," in *U.S. News and World Report* (April 2, 2007), 14.
37. "The Last Temptation of Al Gore," Reviewed by Eric Pooley, *Time* (May 28, 2007), 41.
38. "Relativity Turns 100", *Astronomy Magazine,* February, 2005.
39. Florence Scovel Shinn, *Think Exist.com,* http://thinkexist.com/quotation/intuition_is_a_spiritual_faculty_and_does_not/324095.html, (accessed November 1, 2010).
40. Laurens van der Post, "New York City Department of Parks and Recreation," *Lewis Pasteur Park News.* www.nycgovparks.org/parks/Q369, (accessed November 1, 2010).
41. Alexis Carrel, *Time for Change,* http://timeforchange.org/definition-of-intuition-intuitive.
42. Margery Allingham, from "Death of a Ghost," http://www.brainyquote.com/words/de/deducation151915.html.
43. Gladwell, Malcom, *Outliers, The Story of Success* (Ney York: Penguin Group, 2008): 216–219.

Component Five:

Plan Strategy

Causing a Predictable Reaction

Focus, preparation, toughness of spirit, and a determination to outmaneuver the other are the basic ingredients for successful strategy planning. A negotiation designer shapes the game by influencing what issues are first and when and where to start the negotiation. These skills, linked to a respect for timeless values and for the needs of others, result in negotiating more effectively.

USE THE POWER OF PURPOSE

Planning strategy involves focusing on a specific goal as we use the power of purpose to prepare, plan, and practice. All three endeavors involve a great paradox. On the one hand, they are highly rational and capable of study, yet on the other hand, all three are driven by non-rational dynamics. Our approach, therefore, should be to look for the underlying feelings and interests behind the stated positions of an opponent. Preparing a strategy involves programming our own set of inner signals and prioritizing goals and benchmarks. It involves finding ways to combine forces, interests, and concepts.

In tennis we are told not just to "watch the ball" but to keep an eye on the seams of the tennis ball; it is the spin on the ball that causes a predictable reaction. We utilize imagined experiences as we visualize hitting that cross-court, making that slice down the sideline, and smashing that overhead. The strategy of learning to focus on the ball—on the problem—can be used to give that winner's edge as a negotiator. And we must have a goal because not having one is like shooting without a target.[1]

General Chuck Yeager, the world famous test pilot, warned not to wait for trouble but to think and plan. Seneca (4 BC–65 AD) said: "When one does not know what harbor he is heading for, no wind is the right one." Another way of saying this is that "luck is the residue of design."[2]

Focusing Attention

Concentration is the act of focusing attention. As the mind is allowed to focus on a single object, it stills. As it is kept in the present, the mind calms and focuses on the present situation.[3]

> ***Insights from a Fresh Perspective:*** *The moves the chess master makes when there is something to "do," such as the brilliant sacrifice culminating in checkmate or springing the trap, which captures the enemy queen, is only one aspect of the game. The other arguably more important phase of the game, is "strategy": what the chess master "does" when there is nothing to "do." The game may reach a point when the master has achieved a perfect defensive posture, and any further move inevitably weakens his position; or, he may be prepared for the all-out attack after all his pieces have reached their strongest positions, but the weakness in the enemy camp has not yet revealed itself. In situations like this, the master employs the strategy of the waiting move that confuses the amateur, since it does not seem to accomplish anything.*

Self-awareness is closely related to the power of directing attention. Attention is often captured by outside forces, which we may or may not have chosen (sights, sounds, colors) or by our internal forces (expectations, fears, worries, interests). When our attention is so captured, we function very much like a machine: we are not doing things; they simply happen. However, there continuously exists the possibility that we may take the matter in hand and deliberately direct attention to something entirely of our own choosing, something that does not capture the individual but is captured by the individual. The difference between directed and captured attention is the same as the difference between making things happen and letting things take their course.[4]

Practical Tips

When focusing on money, ask:

- "Why, how, when, and to whom is this money to be paid?"

When performance is an issue, ask:

- "What is to be done?"
- "How is it to be done?"
- "When is it to be done?"
- "What will happen if it is not done?"

Assessing Power Balance

A key element in strategy planning is assessing power balance. This involves not only the actual balance of power between the parties but, more importantly, each party's perception of that power balance. Power, like beauty, is largely a state of mind. In negotiation, perception is the reality. Balance of power includes the balance of rewards, balance of punishment for non-reward, balance of legitimacy, balance of commitment, balance of knowledge, balance of competition, balance of uncertainty and courage, balance of time and effort, and balance of bargaining skills.[5]

Family law negotiation often involves intensified feelings. The best negotiating approach, therefore, is to focus in the beginning on calming emotions. Allow the parties to vent emotional energy before beginning the negotiation. A practicing attorney said, "In family law practice, be confident enough to make a deal . . . try to get everyone comfortable with themselves . . . don't negotiate always as a "bargaining lawyer," but as a businessman getting to the point. Get past this breast-beating and get to the basics. Kids and money are explosive."[6]

In the 2007 football classic between defending national champion, Florida, and LSU, Florida was ahead the entire game until the last few moments. LSU chose to "go for it" on five fourth-down plays and was successful each time. This set up the winning score. Every decision was part of using the power of purpose in strategic planning. LSU put the right spin on their plays to cause a predictable reaction. They correctly assessed power balance by maintaining ball control in order to keep the talented Florida offense off the field. They decided when and how to be aggressive, and, more importantly, they stuck to their game plan as pressure increased. After the game, coach Les Miles commented, "I didn't just roll the dice . . . there are reasons you do or don't do those things: momentum, feel of the game, time of the game. We felt we used plays that would work. There's a feel to what you have to do to win the game."[7]

Tennis champion Chris Evert advises, "Always save the best shots for when they are needed most." This tennis wisdom from Evert is similar to the ancient advice of Sun Tzu in *The Art of War*:

> All men can see the individual tactics necessary to conquer, but almost no one can see the strategy out of which total victory evolves. Military tactics are like water, for water in its natural course runs away from high places and hastens downward. So in war, the way is to avoid what is strong and to strike at what is weak. Water shapes its course according to the nature of the ground over which it flows; the soldier works out his victory in relation to the foe whom he is facing.[8]

President Dwight D. Eisenhower once said, "The older I get, the more wisdom I find in the ancient rule of taking first things first, a process that often reduces the most complex human problems to manageable proportions."[9]

> ***Insights from a Fresh Perspective:*** *The element of surprise, while effective in warfare, is not always a good technique in a negotiation. It is important for the other side to recognize a rational pattern to your offers and talking points. It is advisable to have an alternative strategy that will unleash an unexpected fact or higher/lower than the anticipated offer on the opposing team, but a negotiator's main ally is a reputation as being reasonable. Everyone, in the course of her career, will have good facts on her side, and it will be tempting to use those facts as a nuclear explosion to turn around a negotiation that is not going as planned or kick start a negotiation that has grown stagnant. Sometimes this strategy is advisable, but a negotiator must*

> *not fall for this temptation. Using your best shot only when you really need it is the sole tactic that will keep your reputation intact.*

VERIFYING INFORMATION

Even Santa checks his list twice. All information, internal or external, should, whenever possible, be verified.[10] Beware of "selective perception" wherein there is a tendency to evaluate information in a way that supports our own beliefs, assumptions, and self-image. We tend to discount what is not known in favor of what is known, leading to an optimistic overconfidence in our chances for success. We tend to overvalue things that are certain, while undervaluing probable or speculative outcomes.[11] We need to get the facts straight.

Practical Tips

When planning, ask:

- Who is my opponent?
- What strategy is required?
- When should I be aggressive?
- Why negotiate at this point?
- Where should I negotiate?
- How is my opponent likely to react?

Remember, it is the process of creating a viable plan that is often more rewarding than the plan itself.

Risk Assessing Opponent

The ability to assume risk is relative. An opponent's confidence is largely determined by that opponent's own perception of tolerance for risk. Faced with this situation, our first response tends to be to adopt a position. But avoid attacking the opponent's position; instead, try presenting differing interests. The opponent may feel less threatened if the conflict is not based on identity.[12]

Our opponent wants to feel capable of influencing our behavior. For this reason, our opponent is more likely to make concessions when feeling competent. So if we can find a way to show our opponents that they are regarded as tough and worthy negotiators, perhaps by coordinating a few concessions on relatively minor issues, then it may be possible for us to induce even greater concessions.[13]

> ***Insights from a Fresh Perspective:*** *In Nigeria the ethnic group of the Yorubas have a saying:* "adura mo s`ugbo`n na tele, to`-lehi`n emi" *(I pray but the logic follows me). I discovered in the negotiation proceedings how true this old proverb was. It is not enough to go on feelings; one must draw on the logic gathered from studying the other party. Allowing myself the ability to recognize the logic of my opponent allows me to shift gears when necessary.*

Allowing Enough Time

Many unskillful negotiators place a dysfunctional premium on speed. Concerns often constitute merely a psychological uneasiness about wasting time. Certainly time is valuable, and sometimes we should be willing to trade money against time. Some people, however, are far too impatient and do not allow enough time to consummate a deal, to allow the process to work.[14] In other words, don't rush the process.

Using Imagination to Predict What Is Needed

In preparing, planning, and practicing, a negotiator should use imagination to anticipate and predict what is needed. People are usually far more concerned with what is likely to happen in the near and distant future than with what is actually happening right now. Therefore, exclude some alternatives in advance or run the risk of becoming overwhelmed with possibilities. In other words, predict what is needed at each point, otherwise there will be far too many alternatives from which to choose.[15]

Practical Tips

Decide ahead of time on a reserve position—the point at which you will go no further.

Never " lose because of your own mistakes."[16]

Remember the old saying, "He who rides a tiger can never dismount." And, "The problems of victory are more agreeable than defeat, but no less a problem."[17]

Try finessing tensions that inherently exist

- Between creating and distributing value;
- Between competing and collaborating;
- Between being assertive and showing empathy.

VARY YOUR APPROACH

I noticed a change in my driving style since moving to the mountains of North Carolina from Louisiana. I found that instead of simply pressing the accelerator to speed up or jamming the brake to slow down, it is much more effective speed control to shift down to a lower gear before entering a steep mountain curve. After a little practice, I determined which gear gives the best control and handling.

Similarly, in negotiating, using different strategies and techniques to control the tempo is recommended. This way, we avoid something that causes many people trouble: the tendency to use just one negotiation gear for every situation. Learn to experiment with the subtle effects of using different gears. We ought to look for new ideas outside of our immediate areas of expertise because, as the old saying goes, often it is the wild hare that comes in and finds the solution.

Remember that if we engage in straightforward strategy planning based entirely on a rational, logical approach without stretching our imagination, we may miss some hidden alternatives.

Practical Tips

Take a moment before making a proposal (presenting a price change or non-monetary concession) to package it carefully, explain the facts supporting your interpretation of the situation (the curve in the road ahead). Then, pause (shift to a lower gear), and confidently say what you have to say (take the curve, accelerating).

Using Positive Self-Talk

In planning our strategy, we should use positive self-talk because it has been demonstrated through research that people always move in the direction of their most current, dominant thought.[18] Therefore, focus on doing, not on not doing. Have a goal and do not dwell on the reverse of an idea because optimism is the natural biology of hope, and the mind often cannot distinguish between the negative and positive aspects of an idea.

Showing a Sense of Humor

Former North Carolina Senator Sam J. Ervin, Jr. defines humor as "the faculty of perceiving wisdom and communicating it in amusing or comical ways, which command attention . . . humor makes our heavy burdens light and smooths the rough spots in our pathways. Humor endows us with the capacity to clarify the obscure, to simplify the complex, to deflate the pompous, to chastise the arrogant, to point to a moral, and to adorn a tale."

He also states, "an ounce of revealing humor often has more power to convince than do many tons of erudite argument."[19]

Practical Tip

When I'm playing golf, I try to avoid ever saying to myself "don't hit it into the water" because my mind seems to translate this statement as, "into the water, hit it!"

In negotiating a contract with numbered paragraphs, plan to discuss paragraphs 3, 4, and 5 before paragraph 2 for better timing and more control. Set your own strategy independently of the anticipated order of discussion.

When the other owes expenses, instead of asking for a separate check to cover these expenses, it is better strategy to deduct them and deliver a check for the net amount due.

It is easier to cease doing something (refrain from contacting customers) than to undertake a new course of action (send out change of business notice).

Know your opponent's peculiarities. German General Rommel, sometimes referred to respectfully as the "Desert Fox," wrote about his strategy using armored vehicles. In the movie *Patton*, General Patton, leading his allied forces against Rommel in North Africa during World War II, proclaims, "You magnificent b——, I read your book."

Being Sensitive to Cultural Differences

As international business increases, smart negotiators in the West must overcome cultural barriers in other countries. When encountering great cultural differences, it is often better to negotiate "off the record" and not make every meeting a formal session. Show respect for the other culture, and, above all, be patient. Remember when leaving for Latin America, Africa, or the Middle East to think in terms of Einstein's Special Theory of Relativity: "Time expands. . . . Slow down."[20]

Postponing Decisions When Planning

A systematic approach in strategy planning is achieved by using an analytical framework showing the contours of the problem in a decision tree approach (made famous in the popular game theory analysis by Nobel Prize winner John Nash) where we identify, on a tree diagram, each decision's alternative by a branch depicting possible outcomes and consequences. This helps postpone decisions, spot and define issues, brainstorm with colleagues, and visualize potential solutions. The trick is not to force a quick answer but rather to wait patiently for a well-reasoned solution to emerge. A premature decision closes thinking to other alternatives. It changes focus at this point from exploring options to justifying decisions made. In a sense, our mental database is told, "We are moving ahead on this solution, act accordingly, and send no new ideas."

Taking a Planning Pause

Sometimes it is helpful to gather the facts and then take a pause to postpone the decision for a period while doing something else. The trick is to keep the left-brain (the editor) occupied with some routine activity (driving a car, taking a swim, digging in the garden, taking a walk, or playing golf or tennis), while allowing our right brain to use our informed intuition to create new ideas.

Practical Tip

Consider preparing at least three alternatives to present to your opponent. Only presenting two could be perceived as an ultimatum.

When taking a pause, the trick is, as stated by Ernest Hemingway, not to consciously "think about anything that I was writing from the time I stopped writing until I started again the next day. That way my subconscious would be working on it and at the same time I would be listening to other people and noticing everything."[21]

Since people can look without seeing and hear without listening, isn't it also possible that they can think that they are thinking about a problem when actually they really are not giving it the kind of thought that generates bright ideas, different perspectives, and out-of-the-box solutions?[22] Therefore, when in doubt, take a planning pause.

Adapting an Idea Instead of Copying a Blueprint

In 1905, British naval engineers were commissioned to build a new battleship. They chose to build a battleship that was fast, utilizing huge turbine engines. It was made lighter because it did not use much armor. Britain permitted Japan, its ally at the time, to copy the British blueprints, but arch-rival Germany received nothing more than word that an improvement to the battleship was being made. The Germans had a general idea of battleship improvement but had to work out all of the details themselves, and in constructing their updated battleship, they incorporated much heavier armor and twice the number of watertight compartments. In the famous battle of Jutland on May 31 and June 1, 1916, the British lost more ships and incurred more than twice as many casualties as the Germans. Fast forward to 1942. In the battle of Guadalcanal, the U.S. inflicted heavy casualties on the Japanese fleet built with those same British blueprints.

When choosing a strategy for negotiating, be cautious and always distinguish clearly between copying another negotiator's strategy and running the risk of being left behind by changing facts and technology or, on the other hand, adopting a great idea and reworking the details.

> ***Insights from a Fresh Perspective:*** *Perhaps the most famous criminal negotiation of all time was the Iran Hostage Crisis. The lessons learned from that fateful event changed the course and fortunes of not only the nations involved, but of the world. Short of showing remarkable initial restraint, President Carter made many*

incorrect assumptions about his adversaries; he waffled between strategies, and the administration's actions did not support the rhetoric and public saber-rattling seen in the newspapers and on television. To ally the American people behind him, he persisted in his focus on the hostage crisis and neglected other aspects of government. This strategy backfired, inadvertently placing a higher value on the lives of the American captives, which weakened the U.S. position at the bargaining table. Carter was relying on the Iranians playing by our rules, adhering to our system of values under the time-honored European tradition of détente. Ayatollah Khomeini, by contrast, played his hand to perfection. Concessions, while honorable in the Western tradition, were seen as weakness to the Iranians. Every American overture was exploited and, even though the hostages were eventually released, Khomeini succeeded by ridding his government of moderates and replacing them with fundamental extremists. More importantly, he was able to galvanize anti-American sentiment throughout the Middle East.

PLAN TO STAY IN CONTROL

A great example of emotional control is explained by Reg Pridmore, champion motorcycle racer and instructor who, as he is driving in the rain, reflects on the power of the right hand. He says the most important lesson when driving a motorcycle in the wet is that emotions must be controlled through the throttle hand.[23]

Practical Tips

Recognize feelings and keep in the front of your mind that the goal is to act professionally. This means to listen carefully, to hear what is being said, and to say only what must be said. You might feel uneasy (that an opponent seems too rushed), maybe a little desperate (because if you say something wrong, the chances for settlement might be ruined) or maybe a little aggressive (because of past issues with an opponent). Regardless of these feelings, try to stay focused.

"In representing the defense you can't let your dislike of the other attorney color your case . . . don't respond emotionally to threats . . ."[24]

Shaping the First Offer, the First Concession

"A reasonable offer early on by the defense attorney often saps the incentive of the plaintiff's attorney because the plaintiff's attorney anticipates the amount of work that the defense attorney can generate."[25]

Who makes the first real offer in adversarial negotiations is often not as important as who makes the first concession. This is not just because the first concession in itself is damaging but because it indicates who has the least leverage. Some even suggest that making the first offer can be of tactical advantage because it affords an opportunity to evaluate closely the other side's response. In problem-solving negotiations—competitive or cooperative—making the first offer may influence the adversarial opponent to adopt a joint problem-solving approach.[26]

First offers have a powerful effect on the negotiation environment because they pull judgments toward themselves, producing a strong anchoring effect, even among very experienced negotiators. Studies have shown that aggressively high (but not absurd) listing prices for real estate or asking prices for a used car influence the final price, upward. Furthermore, our opponent's satisfaction often depends on the number and size of concessions extracted from us. Caution in making the first offer, however, is needed when our opponent has the most information or when the opening offer is an enticement as in an auction.[27]

Maintaining Momentum

When winning, do not choke and change an approach just because it becomes suddenly apparent that defeat is possible. Keep the game plan, realizing that if the negotiation is won, we win, and if we lose, the opponent was better. Believe that we can win at a level we have never won before. Go for it! Don't change the game. When we have momentum in a negotiation, it is not wise to stop to analyze the mechanics or to draft the language for implementing subsequent points.[28] It is much better to solve the issue in principle now and draft later. Too many details too soon tend to block creative problem-solving.[29]

Remaining Target-Focused as Pressure Increases

In golf, those who consistently putt better under pressure are not thinking about details such as grip, stance, alignment (left-brain thoughts) but rather about the target and visualizing the ball dropping in the hole (right-brain focus). In negotiating, it is often better strategy to focus on achieving a goal rather than only thinking about all the details involved.

> ***Insights from a Fresh Perspective:*** *When training as a hunter-jumper in horseback riding, you are taught to keep your heels pointed down, your legs in line with your hips, elbows in, shoulders back, and head up. When you approach the jump, you sit deep in the saddle. As you go over the jump, you allow the momentum to bend you in a two-point position and then in an upright position after you land. All of this must be done automatically when you are in a competition surrounded by loud speakers and other distractions. You learn to tune out all distractions and focus only on the jump in front of you.*

Learning from Losing

World-class football quarterback Fran Tarkenton points out that in society, some have led people to believe that there is a strict separation between winners and losers. This is not accurate. If one is in the arena doing things, one is going to lose sooner or later. What distinguishes a winner is how one deals with loss. Winners take their losses and learn from them. That helps make these people smarter, tougher, and stronger, and it inspires them to go forward.[30]

CHANGE ROLES

For a negotiator, role and function vary with the circumstances. Each role has a different purpose, so stay prepared to change roles.

Plan Designer

Since planning gives the highest return for time spent, we might think that the plan, which is established after hours of work and research, is what is most important. But often, it is not the plan itself but the process of creating the plan that is most important. Creating the plan prepares us to expect the unexpected and to look for patterns in the process.

The design plan for a negotiated settlement is similar to the way that architectural drawings lay out the plan for a building. Blueprint designs contain features on two different levels: those which are central to the basic structure of the building (such as load-bearing walls) and cannot be changed without altering the entire design, and those which reflect the individual tastes of the owners (such as the placement of kitchen cabinets) that can be modified to accommodate personal interests.[31]

Information Gatherer

Former senator and prosecutor in the Nixon proceedings Sam J. Ervin Jr. recalled his father's advice to him upon joining his father's firm: "Son, salt down the facts; the law will keep."[32] As an information gatherer, our first focus should be to get the facts straight.

Additional facts by themselves cannot expose opportunities, ideas, or options. Nor can additional facts by themselves help us see the way around problems and corners. None of this can happen if we do not have the right data engine to turn what is assimilated into something that can actually be used.[33] The data engine for the negotiator is the informed intuition.

> **Practical Tips**
>
> Try exploring alternatives while keeping the goal in the forefront. A good approach is to listen to one person/idea at a time. Stay tuned to your informed intuition and don't drown out that small voice. Go for quantity of ideas. Edit later. Make a chart.

Contingency Cataloger

Cataloguing contingencies permits the skilled negotiator to "recognize, minimize, and control risks until the last possible minute," and then to "win and win fast." This involves formulating possible alternative courses of action, testing for what can go wrong, separating negotiable from non-negotiable elements, and "taking the worst scenario and doubling it!"[34]

Planning strategy should also include the best alternative to a negotiated agreement (BATNA), a popular concept developed by Professors Roger Fisher and William Ury of Harvard University in their classic book *Getting to Yes*[35]. When a negotiator says, "I want to be able to walk away," the next question is, "What do I want to walk away to?" What is the best alternative to that negotiated agreement being rejected?

Einstein stated, "If at first an idea doesn't sound absurd, then there is no hope for it. . . . The formulation of the problem is often the most important part of the solution." Remember the old saying: "I change my mind often, but at any given moment I am never in doubt."

Facilitator

Being an effective facilitator requires focusing on solutions. Shakespeare said, "Our doubts are traitors, and make us lose the good we oft might win by fearing to attempt."[36] Henry Ford followed this thought when he stated that he was "looking for . . . [people] who have an infinite capacity for not knowing what can't be done."[37]

An important role of a negotiator is to begin "mining for interests," which is to look for the story beneath issues and positions.[38]

Peacemaker

"Discourage litigation. Persuade neighbors to compromise whenever you can point out to them how the nominal winner is often the real loser in fees, expenses, and wasted time. As a peacemaker, the lawyer has a superior opportunity of becoming a good person."[39]

Implementer

Perhaps the most valuable result of all education and training is the ability to make ourselves do the things that must be done whether we like it or not. This lesson must be learned first, but it is probably the last lesson we learn thoroughly. This skill includes the ability to stay focused on implementing our strategy plan despite unnerving personal remarks aimed at upsetting us. How do we keep our cool and not react?

> ***Insights from a Fresh Perspective:*** *When I am personally attacked verbally, I have learned to treat these attacks as test questions. I have seen those questions previously and already know the answers, so I don't react.*

Strategy Reviewer

Strategic principles alone cannot solve the practical problems with which they are concerned. A practical problem can only be solved by action itself. In other words, we must add something to our strategy concepts to make them applicable to practice. We add our own experience as to a particular situation and, most importantly, judgment of how to apply these concepts. As we take and test these ideas, be sure to apply an ample dose of imagination.

> ***Insights from a Fresh Perspective:*** *When creating a negotiation strategy, a person should not make the plan rigid. A rigid plan is a plan that is set up to be followed precisely like a checklist. Instead, it should be like the Constitution of the United States, flexible enough to be applied to multiple situations.*

While working on strategy, remember that the plan, as implemented, is going to be tested at the end after the negotiations are concluded and we have time to take a learning pause and reflect. We ask ourselves questions such as, "When we created our plan, did we allow enough time for it to incubate? How did the plan compare with what actually transpired during the negotiations? How accurately did the plan anticipate flow of information exchange, pattern of offers and concessions, and final result? How did we handle the professionalism issues Judge Rubin suggested?" This dialogue we create with ourselves, through our informed intuition, is perhaps the most important negotiating strategy to practice and perfect. This dialogue not only helps us establish our values, but also increases our creativity and problem-solving abilities.

> ***Insights from a Fresh Perspective:*** *I have often heard that, when practicing a skill(such as singing or dancing), one should practice as if it is not a practice, but the actual performance. Practicing*

> *half-heartedly may lead to the performance also appearing half-hearted, as the entertainer grew accustomed to the careless means of performing. The same could hold true with negotiations. If one runs through a negotiation in his head, leaving out details, skipping steps, not thinking each angle through, what is to prevent such things from occurring during the actual negotiation?*

As we engage in the review of our strategy, look for conceptual blocks, and identify them. This way, we learn what types of blocks to expect in various situations.[40] As the old saying goes, "recognizing a problem is half of the solution." Also try to include in the strategy plan the use of analogy and metaphor. This helps us see relationships, and serves as a contrast to the tendency in our electronic age to deluge our opponents with data and choke them with choices.[41] We focus on tackling novel challenges instead of solving routine problems.[42]

Also remember that we are all programmed in our thinking, and we tend to have well-developed thinking styles. This means that we all have conceptual blocks. But we have the ability to modify our problem-solving habits in order to arrive at more creative inputs. Problems we face may be obscured by either inadequate clues or misleading information. So the critical first step is to remove our perceptual blocks and try to isolate and define the problem with more conceptual clarity.

We should use all our senses and focus on bringing together two or more ideas that are not ordinarily combined in order to create a little humor.

Strategy planning must be implemented through well-chosen tactics, the subject of our next component. Notice how the two subjects overlap, particularly in the middle of a negotiation, where we must be ready to change our strategy and tactics and, at the end of our negotiation, when we need to evaluate our strategy and tactics.

What strategic patterns have you anticipated?

Summary

- Develop a plan to cause a predictable reaction.
- Prepare a list of questions to ask.
- Anticipate packaging all proposals by giving the reasoning before the price.
- In planning, resist the urge to come to a quick answer; instead, explore a range of alternatives and wait patiently for a solution to emerge.

NOTES

1. Benjamin Franklin, *Guidelines For Great Events,* www.springvillecamp.com/Guidelines%20for%20Great%20Retreats.pdf.
2. Branch Rickey, former owner of Brooklyn Dodgers Baseball Team, www.great-quotes.com/quote/937583.
3. W. Timothy Gallwey, *The Inner Game of Tennis* (New York: Random House, 1989), 9, 35.
4. E.F. Schumacher, *A Guide for the Perplexed* (New York: Harper Perennial, 1978), 67.
5. Gary Bellow, *Lawyering Process: Negotiation* (West Publishing Group, 1981), 22–25.
6. Wayne D. Wykoff, Sexton & Wykoff, PLLC, Attorneys, Knoxville, speaking to the class.
7. *USAToday* (October 8, 2007), 11c.
8. Sun Tzu translated by Samuel B. Griffith, *The Art of War* (Oxford University Press, 1973), 28–29.
9. President Dwight D. Eisenhower, "Wisdom," *Webster's Quotations, Facts and Phrases* (2008), 13.
10. Henry S. Kramer, *Game, Set, Match: Winning the Negotiation Game* (ALM Publishing/ALM Inc., 2001), 33. Kramer is a corporate labor negotiator and professor at Cornwell University.
11. John S. Murray, Alan Scott Rau, and Edward F. Sherman, *Negotiation* (Foundation Press, 1996), 9, 52.
12. Tim Hicks, *Negotiation Journal* (January 2001), 35, 40.

13. Murray, *Negotiation*, 7, 81, 112.
14. Howard Raiffa, John Richardson and David Metcalfe, *Negotiation Analysis: The Science and Art of Collaborative Decision Making* (Cambridge, MA: Harvard University Press, 2003), 150.
15. Frank Smith, *Understanding Reading: A Psycholinguistic Analysis of Reading and Learning to Read*, 6th Ed. (TF-LEA, 2004), 24, 58–59.
16. Tennis Champion Boris Becker, commenting after winning a big watch.
17. Winston Churchill, *Quotations Book*, http://quotationsbook.com/quote/10380/.
18. Adopted from Dr. Dennis Waitely in his tapes on *The Dynamics of Winning*.
19. Sam J. Ervin, Jr., *Humor of a Country Lawyer* (Chapel Hill: University of North Carolina Press, 1994), 5.
20. Ed Brodow, *Negotiation Bootcamp: How to Resolve Conflict, Satisfy Customers, and Make Better Deals* (New York: Currency Double, 2006), 166, 167.
21. Ernest Hemingway, *A Moveable Feast* (NY: Scribner, 1992), 13.
22. James C. Freund, *Lawering: A Realistic Approach To Legal Practice* (Law Journal Seminars-Press, 1979). The reader should pay close attention to Freund's practical, forthright approach in relating example stories in the chapters entitled, "Legal Analysis" and "The Exercise of Good Judgment."
23. Sue Zesiger, "The Wild Bunch," *Fortune*, (June 8, 1998), 314.
24. Brian Trammel, Kennerly, Montgomery & Finley, PC, Attorneys, Knoxville, speaking to the class.
25. John W. Perry, Jr., attorney, Baton Rouge, speaking to the class.
26. Robert M. Bastress and Joseph D. Harbaugh, *Interviewing, Counseling and Negotiating Skills for Effective Representation* (Boston, MA: Little Brown & Company, 1990), 493–97.
27. Ideas adopted from an article by Adam D. Galinsky in *Negotiation* (Harvard Business School, July 2004), 2.

28. D.B.H. Chaffe, III, Chaffe & Associates, New Orleans, speaking to the class.
29. Murray, *Negotiation*, 74, 82.
30. Adopted from Fran Tarkenton, 18 seasons as quarterback for the Minnesota Vikings and the New York Giants, NFL Hall of Fame, quarterback of the Vikings when they lost three Super Bowls, successful businessman who wrote, *What Losing Taught Me About Winning: The Ultimate Guide for Success in Small and Home-Based Business* (Fireside, 1999).
31. Murray, *Negotiation*, 120.
32. Sam J. Ervin, Jr., Murray, *Negotiation*, (Chapel Hill: University of North Carolina Press, 1994), 106.
33. Idea adopted from advertisement for Informix Corporation, 1999.
34. John Hastie, attorney, Oklahoma City, speaking to the class.
35. Roger Fisher and William Ury, *Getting to Yes, Negotiating Agreement Without Giving In* (Boston: Houghton Mifflin, 1992), 19–106.
36. William Shakespeare, *Measure for Measure*, Act I. Scene IV.
37. Henry Ford, *Sayings About Motivation*, www.quotegarden.com/goals.html
38. Idea adopted from Earl Nightingale, *Lead the Field*, "Lesson 1, The Magic, Word and Acres of Diamonds."
39. Abraham Lincoln, "The Lawyer as a Peacemaker," *History Cooperative*, www.historycooperative.org/journals/jala/16.2/steiner.html
40. James L. Adams, *Conceptual Blockbusting, A Guide to Better Ideas* (Reading, MA: Addison-Wesley Books, 1986), 118.
41. Ibid., 218.
42. Daniel H. Pink, *A Whole New Mind, Why Right-Brainers Will Rule the World* (NY: The Penguin Group, 2006), 39–40, 139.

Component Six:

Anticipate Tactics

Being Prepared

Just as strategy deals with the overall plan of the negotiation, tactics focus on implementing strategy. The same ingredients are present: time, power, information, and credibility.

Using only one type of tactic is like coaching a football team only on offense while ignoring defense. Familiarity with various tactics should not be confused with mastery. Beginners and experts use their arsenal of negotiating tactics differently. Experienced negotiators use tactics to explore the possible existence of, and move toward, a mutually beneficial settlement that all can accept.[1]

Having two eyes gives us the ability to see the world in three dimensions with the advantage of added depth perception. In *3D Negotiations,* David Lax and James Sebenius describe negotiating in three dimensions. Those three dimensions are in play concurrently: 1) Tactics build communication and trust; 2) Deal Design creates greater value by dovetailing differences among the parties in a creative way so as to offer value to all sides; and 3) Setup involves taking the proper steps before coming to the table, before tactical interplay begins, to insure that the right parties, sequences, issues, and expectations are present at the right time.[2]

Most things in life have a pattern—a timing. Likewise negotiations have a before, beginning, during, closing, and after—a sequence. People like things in a known order, and when we vary the order or timing, people often get confused, and when they get confused, they are not easily persuaded.

Four elements affect a negotiation: 1) Clients we can't control; 2) Facts we can't control but can develop; 3) Preparation, which is exclusively in our control; and 4) Credibility, which is also exclusively in our control.[3]

To consider these dynamics, it is necessary to pause at each stage of the negotiation sequence (before, beginning, during, closing, after) and examine the strategic tactics that should be used at that particular moment.

BEFORE NEGOTIATIONS

Before negotiations, plan for the future and anticipate what is likely to happen. Become masters of painting future pictures and of providing vision, guidance, and judgment. Before we start negotiations, we must thoroughly understand those whom we are representing in terms of priorities, goals, and values. Consider how they feel. What are their views about short-term economic gain, long-term economic security, and risk-taking? Then we have to prepare them for the negotiation. Do they understand the risks? Do they share the analysis of a realistic goal for settlement? Are they emotionally ready?

First, we decide when (time of day) and where (our office, their office, or a neutral place) to negotiate, what we want to achieve, and what the priorities are. Then we identify issues and make our own agenda, including the anticipated first offer and trade-offs. Next, we analyze our opponent's position, underlying needs, and probable tactics. We then develop a strategy to present our position—not to *prove* we are right, but to *persuade*. We mentally rehearse, etch in the mind's eye the anticipated negotiation, and imprint a mental image of the strategy we have planned. Lastly, we determine the timing of initial proposals and concessions, deadlines, ultimatums, consolidation, and closure.

Practicing attorneys advise that we need to:

- "Get the facts . . . people lie to wives, friends, and lawyers . . . so get the facts . . . don't let your enthusiasm cover your getting facts . . . get the straight story."[4]

- "Know what kind of judge you will be dealing with . . . write that in your mind."[5]
- "Be properly prepared so there is no reason that you can't settle."[6]
- "Prepare for trial if you want to settle. Think only in terms of a trial—send out a brochure and wait ten days. The last thing you want to do as a plaintiff's attorney is rush your case."[7]

Anticipating First Offers

First offers by the seller would normally be the highest that could be reasonably justified. This is referred to as the "anchoring effect." In auctions, however, research has suggested that high opening offers do not lead to high final prices. Given decent interest in an auction item, lower starting prices result in higher final prices—a reversal of the anchoring effect.[8]

> ***Insights from a Fresh Perspective:*** *At the battle of Cannae, the Carthage general Hannibal arrayed his troops in a slight curve. He placed his veterans in the middle and awaited the advance of the Roman army. As the Romans advanced, the middle of Hannibal's line gave ground but the flanks did not. This tactic continued until the Roman army was circled on three sides. At that point, the middle of the line stopped retreating, and the bulk of the Roman army was destroyed. This tactic was risky because had the middle of the line broken, Hannibal's army would have been destroyed. In my own negotiations, I have found that if I give ground where I already know I can, I will be able to hold where I absolutely need to.*

Although it is an old saying that good tactics by themselves can never offset poor strategy, the two are so closely linked that sometimes they are indistinguishable. When riding a highly rambunctious horse, it is suggested the rider use both a bridle and a curb bit. Is that a tactic or a strategy? It makes no difference.

Rex E. Callicott, one of my favorite clients, was both a successful business executive and the owner of five ranches—two for horses and three for cattle. In his later years, while I was discussing estate planning alternatives, he interrupted suddenly and said, "Horse (he often called me Horse instead of Bill), did I ever tell you about the know-it-all that bought a registered quarter horse from me?"

"No, but what does that have to do with the estate plan we are considering right now?"

He said, "Well, I'll tell you. This prospective buyer showed up one day, picked out a horse, grabbed a saddle, and mounted. 'Wait,' I said, 'this horse is not fully broken, and it would be better to have a different bit.' The buyer said, 'No, that's not necessary. I know how to handle a horse.'"

Mr. Rex explained that the ride out into the pasture was well controlled, but on the return, the horse put the bit in its teeth, lowered its head, and sped like a race horse to the barn, around a corner, and under a low beam just above the rider. "When I put my hand on the saddle it was completely wet. Horse, do you know what I'll never forget from that? Well, I'll tell you—when you are heading for the barn, always ride the horse with a tight rein." Mr. Callicott had made his point.

> ***Insights from a Fresh Perspective:*** *Control is power. The negotiator should control as many aspects of the negotiation as possible. Several things cannot be controlled: the client, the facts, and the opposing party's tactics. The negotiator can gain advantage by exercising control over those things that are controllable: your own demeanor, your reactions, and "what if" responses. Control is the product of preparation. Control not only helps the negotiator feel at ease, it also sends an unmistakable, non-verbal message to the opponent that his position may not be as strong as he originally thought.*

Avoiding Putting Yourself in a Corner

Give thought to the seating configuration. Would it be better to sit on the same side (to facilitate viewing something together) or across a table from one another (respecting the private space of each other)? In any case, we don't want to put ourself in a corner where we can't get out. My grandfather, who was a lawyer and district attorney in a rural area of Louisiana from the 1880s until the 1930s, warned his son, who started his practice in New Orleans in the 1920s, "Son, never place your desk up against the wall where you cannot escape if someone comes after you!" My father gave me this very same bit of advice when I began my law career.

> ***Insights from a Fresh Perspective:*** *As a coach, I find athletes begin to compete for the wrong reasons when using consequences as the sole motivator. Using consequences has been proven to motivate people, but I find that if you're focusing on a consequence, then your mind-set is already on the negative side. If you are thinking negatively, you have already lost the battle. Therefore, when preparing for a negotiation, you must not dwell on the consequences of your actions. Instead, think positively and set yourself up for success.*

Practical Tips

Determine where to start negotiating—your office, their office, a neutral place, at a desk, or at a round or rectangle table (a major issue for Henry Kissinger before negotiating for resolution of the Vietnam War). In every case, it is your job to be aware of the effect of the physical surroundings. Be sure to do all of the following prior to beginning the negotiation:

- Have a good breakfast.
- Get the facts straight, including motives.
- Identify issues.
- Make your own agenda including information-producing questions and possible opening offer.
- Analyze opponents' position, needs, emotions.
- Review what has happened to the opponent recently.
- Decide how to start negotiating—in person, telephone, letter, fax, e-mail, or text messaging.
- Break down large or complex issues into smaller, more manageable parts. Remember that complexity is independent of importance. Try not to exceed five items, but it is better to stick to three.
- Use the vividly imagined experience to rehearse and etch in the mind's eye an anticipated negotiation wherein you listen attentively, and then present the reasons and questions followed by your position (and needs), not to prove you are right, but to persuade.

BEGINNING NEGOTIATIONS

In the beginning, while exploring alternatives, separate inventing from deciding. Invent options and brainstorm without committing. Carefully commit later.[9]

At the outset, effective negotiating in complex cases requires separating people from the substantive interests. Often negotiators make the mistake of letting personal animosities influence their bargaining.[10] Consider using the beginning of the negotiations as a fact-finding session where bits and pieces of information are exchanged rather casually. This is time to listen and observe. The beginning is not the time for debate; a well-worded question is probably the most effective tool we have. Try to take charge of the negotiations by using an imaginative counter offer to the original demand.[11]

Use the power of silence. A musician observed that in music, "many handle the notes no better than other pianists; but the pauses between the notes—ah, that is where the art resides."[12] Focus on using terms and conditions generic to the particular negotiation. Be sure to negotiate in the language of the currency.[13]

And, most importantly, be ready to react effectively in unpredictable moments.

> ***Insights from a Fresh Perspective:*** *Rigid and inflexible negotiators lack the requisite relaxation component needed to focus. When I worry too much about the details of my tactics, I lose focus on the priorities. I need to "get a grip," but I find that the most effective grip is a loose one. As the rock band .38 Special used to sing, "Hold on loosely, but don't let go. If you squeeze too tightly, you're gonna lose control."*

Clarifying Capacity

Clarifying the capacity of one person to act on behalf of another is one of those points best explored at the beginning. If we wait to raise this point, it could send an unwarranted signal that something is missing. For example, is the owner/manager of the small company selling a product going to be personally liable for the veracity of all representations and warranties? If there is to be no personal liability, it should be stated. Also, check the language in the power of attorney or the company resolutions passed by its board of directors to determine extent of authority.[14]

Using Small Talk

Part of our beginning tactic is to find out all we can about our opponents. Are they confident, uptight, or laid back? Did they have breakfast and lunch? Are they burdened with other problems? What is their training, background, and religious belief? Are they worried about a check bouncing, making their next appointment, or catching a plane? What do they do for fun? Are they optimistic? Much of this information can be gleaned from the small talk that comes at the beginning of every negotiation.

Exploring Interests behind Stated Positions

Discuss each other's perceptions. Make them explicit in a frank, honest manner. It is common in a negotiation to treat as unimportant those concerns of the other side perceived as not standing in the way of an agreement. To the contrary, communicating loudly and convincingly things we are willing to say that they would like to hear can be one of the best tactics we can use.[15] As the negotiation matures, identify areas our side does not care much about and use these areas to begin making concessions. Try to avoid using only positional bargaining rather than exploring the other's needs and wants. Remember the warning: If the only tool we have is a hammer, every problem is seen as a nail.

Looking for Interests Shared

Harvard Professors Roger Fisher and William Ury teach negotiators to be on the lookout for interests shared with the opponent despite conflicting positions.[16] A merger and acquisition expert advises us to "keep it as simple as possible. Identify areas of agreement and write down what is agreed to. Start with a simple letter of understanding, and, if possible, get it on one page with plenty of white."[17] A rocket engineer asserts, "We can lick gravity, but sometimes the paperwork is overwhelming."[18]

Practical Tips

Explore alternatives and get more facts. Discuss the desired formats and procedure. Pause. (When you control the agenda, you have the advantage of "ball possession" as in football, keeping your offense on the field.)

Separate inventing from deciding where you invent options without committing ("Have you considered . . . ?") Use the "what if" and "would you consider" approach.

Change the subject to maintain control. To avoid discussing something out of sequence, say, "we will come back to that."

Pause before answering questions.

Bring a pocket calculator.

Keep it simple.

Take a break at the right moment in order to maintain control of the tempo, and don't linger in the room.

Postpone making an offer. Focus rather on building a relationship—setting the tone in the first few seconds when a person reacts to the first impression, similar to the pupil of the eye reacting to a change in light. Draw out information by asking probing questions—smoking out concessions. Use questions knowing that negotiation is a process of discovery: "A prudent question is one-half of wisdom."[19]

> ***Insights from a Fresh Perspective:*** *Cyril Connolly wrote, "Hate is the consequence of fear; we fear something before we hate it." Hatred can be the most powerful of all emotions. Hatred can motivate people to do things that are illogical, foolish, morally and ethically wrong, and impossible. Franklin D. Roosevelt so eloquently stated, "The only thing to fear is fear itself." This statement could not be truer in negotiations. Fear can monopolize a negotiation. Fear will define the beginning, the bargaining chips, and the final agreement. Fear leads to hesitation, apprehension, confusion, and ultimately, poor decision-making. Fear must be contained; it must be overcome through preparation, experience, and confidence.*

DURING NEGOTIATIONS

While the beginning phase involves sparring for advantage, and the closing is heavily influenced by time pressures, this middle phase is a time primarily for using measured movement, developing a reasoned approach, and remaining ready for the unexpected.

Using Measured Movement

There is a bag full of practical advice for the negotiator in the middle of negotiations. Perhaps the most important concept is to continue to look for, and be sensitive to, the interests of the opponent still hidden behind stated positions. Others include

- Be definite: "This is something I can recommend to my client."[20] Try to resolve simpler issues first to develop a momentum of progress and trust.
- "Never bid against yourself . . . once an offer is on the table, wait for a counter offer."[21]
- Package concessions with good reasons first so that the opponent will listen carefully and not "shut you off" as soon as the concession figure is given.
- Determine frequency and relative size of concessions. Avoid early concessions as they raise opponent's expectations.
- Give alternatives and set deadlines for offers to expire.
- Make the last concession small and conditioned upon agreement.
- Always remember that those who expect more get more. As in tennis, determine where the ball is to land. Aim, hit, and hang loose with controlled relaxation.
- Listen carefully for offers and hints of offers; look for cues and signals.

Practical Tips

Cushion any counter-move with a cooperative 'signal' or softener to diffuse the sharpness of the reply. Use power when appropriate. Remember that it is more effective to use the hint of power rather than power itself.[22]

> ***Insights from a Fresh Perspective:*** *I keep finding myself thinking back to one of the most important skills a magician can use to pull off his "magic": misdirection. There seems to be a strong analogy between the magician and the negotiator. Both seek to complete their objective successfully without the person on the other side realizing their chosen technique. In both cases, if the other side is able to recognize a pattern in the approach, the chance of success diminishes rapidly. Thus it becomes important to get the other side looking in a different direction, while you skillfully complete your task. The trick is to lead them down the path, and allow them to think they are making the decision of which way to turn, when in fact they are choosing the pre-selected turns you have artfully suggested to them. Hide your competitive style in the cloak of cooperation and allow your competitor to think he has chosen a random card from the deck.*

"It is only proper if you prepare yourself to walk away."[23] To remove unresolved but non-critical issues, consider withdrawing one of yours for one of theirs, like swapping men in checkers or chess. Remember the advice of the King of Siam in the musical *The King and I*: "People are very quick to fight to prove that what they do not know is so."

> ***Insights from a Fresh Perspective:*** *Napoleon Bonaparte, one of history's most famous generals, once said, "Take time to deliberate, but when the time for action has arrived, stop thinking and go in." This quote sums up most of the principles I have learned in negotiations. The first is to prepare: thinking about strategy before the negotiation speaks volumes for your attitude and state of mind during the negotiation. If you are well prepared, you have considered yours and your opponent's arguments and have anticipated reactions from your opponent. You will be able to negotiate without bias, emotion, and insecurity. The second is to use your intuition: when Napoleon says, "Stop thinking and go in," it implies that you are to trust your preparation and go with your instinct. A good negotiator knows to trust intuition when deciding whether to accept, make, or decline an offer. If these principles are followed, then another quote from Napoleon will become appropriate: "What a beautiful fix we are in now; peace has been declared."*

Developing a Reasoned Approach

Emotions are very effective in negotiating, but keep them under control, and, instead, use a reasoned approach. When our emotions are around, our brain wants to take orders from them. This could impair the ability to separate reasons from excuses.

When buying a car, beware. I had to follow my own advice years ago when buying my first BMW. I had researched every article I could find about white station wagons with good gas mileage, low repairs, and traction in both rear wheels for going in the pasture. I was on the verge of buying another Volvo (I had owned five Volvo station wagons over a thirty-five year period) without separate rear wheel traction. Guess what I found out in two phone calls? BMW had just started making station wagons, and few people knew this. The owner of the dealership had a white one with limited slip differential and new-car warranty. And BMW was in a well-publicized race to pass up Mercedes by the end of the quarter, ten days away. When arriving at the dealership, I decided not to even look at the car because he would read me like a book and win an advantage. I thought, "This salesman talks to seven purchasers in a morning; I talk to a car salesman once every seven years.". I tried to offset emotion and adopt a more reasoned approach by saying, "Look, the car doesn't matter, only the price." I then left, not to return until the deal was made. After two days of haggling on the phone, I bought the car for a price lower than a Volvo. Talk about a great car! It did almost everything but cook dinner at the end of the day. And it is still in the family eighteen years later with over 290,000 miles.

> ***Insights from a Fresh Perspective:*** *John Quincy Adams once said, "Patience and perseverance have a magical affect before which difficulties disappear and obstacles vanish." This quote rings true for negotiations. Patience creates a calming, cooperative environment in which you and your opponent can resolve differences and come to a successful conclusion. Patience is not a sign of weakness; rather it is leverage you can use to think critically about your opponent's argument and gain insight into the best resolution for both sides.*

Practical Tips

Continue exploring interests behind stated positions.

Give your opponent a choice between alternatives and be specific by using precise, not rounded, numbers. When possible, use independent criteria to justify the numbers.

Use the power of silence—pause and listen. Allow your opponent to proceed at his/her own pace. Be patient and allow "acceptance time" because time (the hidden language of negotiations) talks.

Remember Thomas Jefferson walking through his garden and saying to himself, "I must try to clear my mind as I approach a plant so that I can be polite and let the plant speak first."

Relax and laugh a little.

Continue to apply the pressure and don't let up until the ninth inning is over.

Use change of pace like a baseball pitcher. Try an "out of character" speech that uses strong but planned emotion.

Use limited authority tactics as a source of control. Consider taking a short tactical recess (like a time out before an important play in football) and change the subject upon returning.

Be ready to suggest the time and place of the next meeting.

Remaining Ready for the Unexpected[24]

Throughout our negotiation experiences, we learn the importance of anticipating and being ready for the unexpected changes that require us to adapt, adjust, and refocus. We ask ourselves if our initial assumptions, made during our strategy planning before or at the beginning of negotiations, are still valid. Our initial plans and strategies, while perfectly reasonable at the time they were made, may now need to be updated to fit changed circumstances because there is now a different type of deal on the horizon than originally envisioned. We not only sense when this change is called for (by noticing surfacing incongruities between the spoken word and the non-verbal signals of the other), but, more importantly, we know what the change should be and how to make it. We do this because we have created a broad base of possible alternatives in our informed intuition.

This is a good time not only to engage in mindful reflection and critical questioning of earlier beliefs but also an appropriate time to take a break and create a safe space (not in front of the opponent) to do it. Being an improviser in the middle of a negotiation requires that we have confidence in our ability to cope regardless of the people, the problem, or the process in place. This redesign function is closely tied to the post-negotiation evaluation we consider at the end of this component.

CLOSING NEGOTIATIONS

After days, even years, of negotiating, often an agreement is reached in just a few minutes. Be conscious of the end approaching (as in football after the two-minute warning) and know there is less time to correct mistakes. If no real deadline exists, consider creating one. In applying this end-game pressure, try not to be the "first to blink." "Show opponents you can hear and explain their case better than they can."[25]

Delay giving monetary figures. Avoid using rounded numbers; instead, use exact numbers based on calculations. Consider referring to outside criteria to determine amounts. Allow the more knowledgeable party to set the first closing offer. Remember Shakespeare's statement: "He is well paid that is well satisfied." The objective is to achieve a fair agreement, not a dead opponent.

Continue to focus on covering all the details. Give reasons for final offer, be specific, and condition it on settlement. Be sensitive to people's tendency to have second thoughts about a major decision just after committing to that decision. So, after finishing negotiations, leave. This is where exit strategy is so important.

"Next to knowing when to seize an advantage, the next most important thing is to know when to forego an advantage."[26] Be aware of seeking the best conclusion without driving too hard a bargain that could haunt later. Compare these two approaches: President Lincoln's treatment of the South after the Civil War was to "let 'em up easy"; the treaty of Versailles after World War I was so harsh that it formed the impetus in Hitler's rise to power.

At the end, we must avoid a distorted image of what the final settlement should look like. It is not like a crescendo, rising to a peak of noise and fury until, with a clash of cymbals, a Settlement is achieved, after which the orchestra's efforts ebb away and everyone goes home. Instead, we should visualize a ripple effect that we get by tossing a stone into a pond.[27]

Practical Tips

Avoid "take it or leave it" and backing opponents into a tight corner with little to lose. They can be transformed into twice the tiger they normally are.

Use the Consumer Price Index (CPI) or other outside standards instead of arbitrary price increases.

Be ready to say, "Let me get back to you." Be accurate with your signals; "This is my best offer" (signaling a nearing of the reserve position); "This is my last offer" (signaling that the final offer is almost here); and "This is my final offer" (signaling that's it, no more).

Focus on being polite and giving the best explanation possible. Allow time for opponents to verify information. Have a credible reason for leaving when you want to.

Listen attentively, (see Component Four, Listen With Four Ears). Use stories to show how other competent and respected people have made similar choices.

AFTER NEGOTIATIONS

Part of strategy and tactics planning includes preparing a list of scripted responses for contingencies, particularly those posing the most threatening possibilities. Then, after negotiations, compare scripted responses with what actually happened. Leading lessons learned are added back into the process. The learning experience is accelerated.

Encouraging a Dialogue with Ourselves

This is when we reflect, take time to develop a keen dialogue with ourselves, and plan how we would do it differently next time. For example, review what factors were most influencing during the negotiation, what were the surprises, what did opponents do that enhanced or weakened their position, and what induced the parties to reach an agreement? This post—negotiation dialogue is one of the most important tactics of an effective negotiator. It is similar to the "pause and learn" sessions of the National Aeronautics and Space Administration, or what the U.S. military calls an "after-action review."

> ***Insights from a Fresh Perspective:*** *In the military, one of the most important aspects of training is the After Action Review (AAR), in which the entire mission is analyzed step-by-step in order to evaluate the performances during each phase. Carver and others stress that a self-AAR is beneficial after negotiations and is an essential step in learning from past experiences. Instead of just mentally reviewing the negotiation, it is best to use a detailed checklist and actually make notations for further references.*

Practical Tips

Follow up to be sure the settlement agreement is unambiguous and is properly executed.

Refrain from any extraneous comments about the settlement. When finished, put the documents and checks in the file, shake hands, and leave as soon as possible.

Continue to be civil and courteous to opponents.

Within a short period, debrief what worked, what the surprises were, and what could have been done differently.

Chair-Flying It to Discover Leading Lessons Learned[28]

All effective strategies and tactics begin with a strong, vivid picture in the mind's eye—a visualization of what we hope to achieve. The widespread use of visualization also creates high performance in competitive sports of all kinds, from the wide receiver in football to the figure skater, to the gymnast, to the golfer. Fighter pilots call this visualization "chair flying." The pilot, sitting in a chair, imagines his hands on the throttle, and goes through the proposed mission to see if it works. Anyone can benefit from this. Before making an important phone call that will begin the negotiation process, chair-fly it. And after negotiations, chair-fly it again, testing plans, rerunning strategy, and fixing tactical flaws. Notice how the little things, repeated over time, form a pattern and make the biggest difference. This debriefing process soon becomes a catalyst to accelerate experience, and gives a better chance to use and transform undesirable things into a successful process. The key here is learning how to manage extremes, how to remain flexible enough to loosen structures to encourage spontaneous creativity, and how to tighten structures enough to keep on track. "To err is human, to err without briefing and debriefing the plan is suicide."[29]

One of my wisest engineer-trained clients, John W. Barton Sr., was a master business deal maker. He always insisted on reviewing in detail the negotiation steps used after every completed transaction. He did this because it worked.

> ***Insights from a Fresh Perspective:*** *Experience without benefit of post-transaction evaluation is of limited value. Ms. Robinson, my high school photography teacher, forced her students to use this post-transaction evaluation technique. As part of the shooting assignments, we had to take the camera off automatic and manually set it for each shot and keep a journal. For each shot number, we showed the time of day, the weather, the F-stop (the diameter of the lens opening which determines how much light is available for the film), the shutter speed, and the film speed. After we developed our photographs, we had to review each shot with the journal to learn what combinations of settings worked for a particular shot at a certain time of day.*

Seeing How We Would Do It Differently

In our review of leading lessons learned, it is helpful to consider what tactics we could have used differently to achieve our strategy plan. Consider using more open-ended questions to gain information before committing. This is an approach proven to be successful in mediation, and it is an equally effective approach in negotiation, as we will consider in our next and final component of Part III.

What patterns have you noticed in your and in the other's tactics?

Summary

- "If good things come to those who wait, imagine what might come to those who prepare?"[30]
- Prior to negotiations, focus on getting the facts straight, anticipating the other's approach, and making your own agenda.
- Begin negotiations by using small talk to explore and look for shared interests.
- During negotiations, be ready for the unexpected; give an opponent a choice between alternatives, using specific, not round, numbers.
- When closing negotiations, be specific, conditioning the last offer on acceptance, but avoid using the "take it or leave it" tactic.
- After negotiations, debrief and look for leading lessons learned.

NOTES

1. David Churchman, *Negotiation: Process, Tactics, Theory* (Lanham MD, University Press of America, 1995), 6.
2. David A. Lax and James K. Sebenius, *3-D Negotiation: Powerful Tools to Change the Game in Your Most Important Deals* (Cambridge, MA: Harvard Business School Press, 2006), 9–13.
3. James P. Roy, attorney, Lafayette, Louisiana, speaking to the class.
4. Arthur Cobb, attorney, Baton Rouge, speaking to the class.
5. Justice Fred Blanche, Louisiana Supreme Court, speaking to the class.
6. Judge Carlos G. Spaht, Baton Rouge, speaking to the class.
7. Michael C. Palmintier, attorney, Baton Rouge, speaking to the class.
8. Adam Galinsky, *New York Times Magazine* (December 10, 2006), 59. The first real offer is often not as important as the first concession; Charles Thensted, *Litigation and Less: The*

Negotiation Affirmative (59 Tul. L. Rev., 1984), 76, 127.

9. Professor Roger Fisher, Harvard Law School, speaking at the Harvard Program on Negotiation.
10. Adopted from Richard Reuben in *ABA Journal,* June 1995.
11. U.N. Hostage Negotiator heard on public radio, December 1999, concerning airline hijacking.
12. Artur Schnabel, quoted by Sydney J. Harris, *It's the Pause That Counts* (Chicago Daily News, 11 June 1958), 18.
13. M. Frank Woods, *Architect,* London, England, commenting on this section.
14. William H. McClendon, III, "Louisiana's New Matrimonial Regime Law: Some Aspects of the Effect on Real Estate Practice" in *Louisiana Law Review* 39, no. 2 (Winter, 1979), 441–77.
15. Roger Fisher and William Ury, *Getting To Yes: Negotiating Agreement Without Giving In,* 2nd Ed. (Boston: Houghton Mifflin, 1992), 40–43, 52, 54–55.
16. Professors Roger Fisher and William Ury of Harvard, speaking at their Program on Negotiation.
17. D.B.H. Chaffe, III, Chaffe & Associates, New Orleans; speaking to the class.
18. Werner Von Braun, famous rocket engineer, NASA, *Oral History and the Contemporary Past Journal* 2, no. 30 (2003): 111–28.
19. Sir Francis Bacon, *Quotations Book,* http://quotationsbook.com/quote/33367/.
20. Vincent P. Fornias, attorney, Baton Rouge, speaking to the class.
21. Donna Wright Lee, attorney, Baton Rouge, speaking to the class.
22. Howard Raiffa, John Richardson and David Metcalfe, *Negotiation Analysis: The Science and Art of Collaborative Decision Making* (Cambridge, MA: Harvard University Press, 2003), 289, 197, 298, 301, 304, 372–74.
23. Hans Sternberg, Baton Rouge, speaking to the class.
24. Many ideas for this section were adapted from an article by Brooks C. Holton, et al, *Negotiation Journal* 26, 69–92.

25. Professor Roger Fisher, Harvard Law School, speaking at the Program on Negotiation.
26. Benjamin Disraeli, *The Quotations Page* http://www.quotationspage.com/quote9066.html
27. As pointed out by mediator, Christopher Honeyman, *Negotiation Journal* 17 (January 2001): 7.
28. "Chair Flying" adopted from, James D. Murphy, *Flawless Execution: Use the Techniques and Systems of America's Fighter Pilots to Perform at Your Peak and Win the Battles of the Business World* (New York: Regan Books, 2006), 95–96.
29. Ibid., 155–57.
30. From an advertisement by The Hartford in *The Sunday New York Times Magazine* (August 26, 2007), 14–15.

Component Seven:

Apply Mediation Principles

Using the Open-ended Question as a Negotiation Tactic

A key interaction exists between negotiation and mediation. Both, along with arbitration, constitute Alternative Dispute Resolution (ADR) procedures for settling disputes other than by litigation. But the non-adversarial, cooperative, problem-solving approach found in mediation can be a most effective tactic for negotiators. Mediation is a term used to describe the intervention of a third party in the negotiation process. The principles of mediation, nevertheless, can be used very effectively in negotiations without third-party assistance. Expanding negotiation tactics to include mediation principles is our last component in Part II, "Becoming More Skilled." It embodies all of the communication subtlety and finesse needed for Part III, "Being More Persuasive."

APPLY MEDIATION APPROACHES

A purely adversarial or position-based approach in negotiations does not always work, while the mediation approach almost always proves effective. For this reason, the mediation principles involved in collaborative, interest-based, or problem-solving negotiation often are used as an alternative to conventional negotiations where adversaries often seek more to win than to solve a problem.[1] In a tough negotiation, a mediator is often needed to help resolve differences. But this may not always be possible. So, in the absence of a third party, the innovative negotiator uses mediation principles to mediate the negotiation.

A key quality in mediation is for the parties to look on themselves as partners, not adversaries. In China, negotiators are called "cooperators," and mediation is viewed as the "first-best" way to settle disputes.

Former Secretary of State Cyrus Vance (1977–1980) was known to the press as an extremely unquotable public figure. What made him a tough interview made him a good mediator. Because he had so little interest in getting credit, the contending parties were more likely to trust him. Vance's recipe was to master the facts of the situation, listen exhaustively to both sides, understand their positions, make sure they understand the principles that must dictate a solution, and never give up.

By Being Aware of the Mediator Mind-set

It is easy to underestimate the amount of uncertainty inherent in problems needing resolution: the law may be unsettled; the facts may be muddled; the nature of the parties and how they will react may be unpredictable. A good mediator wades through the conflicting facts and feelings, unravels the problem, poses alternatives, and leads the parties through all the uncertainty and conflict to a solution. Often the conflict has muddied the lens through which the parties view their problems. In mediation, the safe harbor of a private caucus meeting and the mediation approach affords the opportunity for the parties to clear up their vision by venting feelings, reconsidering alternatives, asking questions, and looking at the argument from different perspectives.

While working through mediation experiences, note the importance of listening well, being creative, using common sense, and exercising sound judgment. All of these attributes, while readily exposed in the mediation process, are often hidden in the competitive negotiation process. Using the mediation approach in negotiating helps us see more realistically where an opponent is coming from, exposing new possibilities for settlement.

By Trusting the Process

Mediation, like negotiation, is enveloped by a process, which, surprisingly, almost always works. Emotions and feelings can sometimes be more important than other facts. As in cooking, when we start with cold ingredients that need to be warmed up, in mediation, feelings and emotions must be gently dealt with. In mediation, the private session is used to encourage the parties to talk about their emotions, to take the lid off and let the steam out. Just as we can't completely control the taste of what is being cooked, we can't completely control the emotions of others. But we soon learn that in either situation, we need to be careful with our seasoning.

At every moment, a mediator must listen intently and observe carefully for facial expressions and other nonverbal signs indicating progress toward a resolution. People often feel that progress is always made in a constant, consistent manner. But this is not so in negotiations and in mediations where change often happens rapidly. Quantum physics teaches us that things do not change slowly over time—they make quantum leaps in a short time.

Practical Tips

The use of "what if" questions by the mediator can be very helpful. What if this should happen? What if a court should hold such and such? What if the measure of damages were changed by this? Is it possible that a future business relationship with your opponent has a dollar value that must be included?

By Distinguishing Efficiency from Effectiveness

Efficiency is doing things right; effectiveness is doing the right things. Trying hard, researching the law, staying focused, and using the right tactics are good habits for the negotiator but never a substitute for judgment. Good judgment involves more than picking the course of action likely to achieve the desired result; it is also the ability to reject the wrong course of action, no matter how appealing it may be.

By Using Questions in the Right Way

The mediator "lives in the question." Open-ended and non-threatening questions expose needed facts and feelings. The mediator listens carefully to detect feelings and interests beneath stated positions.

It is better to ask open-ended questions ("How do you feel about this?") instead of pointed questions that can be answered yes or no ("You feel this matter should be settled now, don't you?").

It is easier to focus on receiving and sending accurate messages decoded from an opponent's style. If an opponent is number-oriented (an engineer, CPA, CFA), speak to the opponent in terms of specific numbers (not rounded) based on independent criteria.

The goal of the mediator is to use questions—not to cause the parties to change their minds about a case but instead to have the parties rise above the case itself, to gain perspective, and to resolve their own differences with a non-adversarial approach. A mediator is a negotiation facilitator who suspends judgment and helps the parties recognize the value of a mutually satisfactory settlement. Mediation works because of the process, not because of the people involved. The mediator's focus, therefore, is on the process, allowing time for the parties to determine the content.

> ***Insights from a Fresh Perspective:*** *A mediator is like a magician because he must devise a settlement plan that looks good to all parties while incorporating factors that are often overlooked. A skilled mediator must recognize the intricate details of a particular fact pattern and realize what emotional baggage is attached to each of these things in order to assure the parties feel satisfied and that they have maintained integrity.*

By Recognizing Personality Traits

Scholars researching the effect that personality traits can have on counseling, interviewing, and negotiating, point out that a person with low tolerance for risk may be tempted to reject strategies with substantial risk elements, even when goals cannot be fully accomplished without more risk-taking. Conversely, a few believe they are "lucky" and enjoy the thrill of high-risk strategies. Both of these situations can be controlled if the mediator has the self-knowledge to recognize the non-strategic factors at work and to limit their influence. Good strategy most often results from calm reflection.

> ***Insights from a Fresh Perspective:*** *Like a sailor guided by the North Star, mediation requires that you trust things that seem*

unreliable. After all, the North Star is so far away. How could it possibly point you in the right direction? The answer is that the North Star is a fixed point. If you trust it, your navigational bearing will be correct. In the world of mediation, issues, clients, and cases change, but your reliance upon your instinct, the mediator, and the truthfulness of your opponent are more constant. Sailing by those fixed points can make for a pretty enjoyable cruise.

By Preserving Relationships

Two businessmen each realized the importance of resolving their dispute and wanted do so in a way that effectively furthered their business interests. Their lawyers were excellent at their craft, but they were concerned with winning the case, not with obtaining a result that made sense. They chose not to use mediation. Instead, they zealously safeguarded the litigation posture of their respective clients and ignored their clients' urgent business needs, which included a desire to preserve a business relationship. These disputants, perhaps, would have been better off if the advocacy plied on their behalf had included an ADR strategy.[2]

Insights from a Fresh Perspective: *The great writer Maya Angelou once stated, "People will forget what you said, people will forget what you did, but people will never forget how you made them feel." This quote holds true particularly so in negotiations. In mediation, taking on the various roles of the parties involved allows us to see all sides of the process. Knowing how others feel gives us a heightened sense of our actions and the effects of those actions on others.*

By Creating Space

Mediation takes place without prejudice. The parties are free to accept or reject any settlement proposal and if not settled, the parties can proceed as if the mediation had not taken place. It is not "on the record." What has been said in the mediation cannot be used as evidence in a trial. The parties are encouraged, therefore, to create space to freely discuss all issues and vent their feelings.

Mediation requires the parties to stop and concentrate on one dispute for an extended period of time, much more than is normally possible in an office setting. The parties become players; they are encouraged to participate and to see that there may be another side to the story. Mediation brings the parties to the bargaining table, educates the participants, and lets the mediator work behind the scenes to develop a settlement.[3]

By Using Opening Remarks[4]

While serving as a mediator in Baton Rouge with Mediation and Arbitration Professional Systems, Inc. (MAPS), I gained experience in using opening remarks in the beginning of the meeting to set the stage for the mediation. During the opening remarks, it is best not to ask questions. Questions asked in the joint meeting (in the presence of all parties) tend to put the one questioned on the defensive. Instead, it is best to start the questioning in the private caucus and allow time for the parties to settle down and get comfortable. Non-threatening questions can be very effective to show willingness to cooperate.

Practical Tips

In the opening joint session, be very brief (two to three minutes maximum). Do not mention settlement numbers. Instead, save these for the private caucus where there is a safe harbor. Avoid putting one party on the spot in front of another.

The following is a sample of opening remarks I use:

"Good morning, I'm Bill McClendon, and I will be conducting this mediation for you. I don't know everyone around the table, so I would appreciate your introducing yourself. I am passing around a sign-in pad.

"First, I want to congratulate all parties for choosing the mediation process. Some of you are probably familiar with mediation, but for others it may be a new experience. This is a voluntary process wherein no decision will be reached without everyone's agreement. Furthermore, all information—all communications and records made and my role during this mediation—are confidential and cannot be used in a trial. This is confirmed in the mediation agreement being signed.

"As a mediator, I am serving as a neutral intermediary only—not as an attorney—not as an advocate for any party. My fee is not based on the outcome and will be paid equally by the parties unless you agree otherwise.

"The procedure today will involve first a joint session, where each of you will be given the opportunity to tell, briefly, what you think is important to consider in settling this dispute. I ask that everyone extend the courtesy to the other of no interruptions or questioning and that you refrain from mentioning any settlement figures at this time. This will come later in the safe harbor of the private caucuses with each party. These private caucuses will be a time to discuss your desires about settlement. All information discussed in this mediation will remain confidential and undisclosed to the other party unless otherwise instructed. I ask you to be frank and candid in assessing and previewing the alternative (likely trial outcome) if this dispute is not settled at this mediation.

"I am committed to spend the day here as your mediator to help you reach your agreement, and I presume each of you is likewise so committed. (I pause and look at each to wait for a nod.)

"During these sessions, I will have to play Devil's Advocate and ask some tough questions. I am not a judge, not acting as a lawyer, but a mediator. So please, 'don't shoot the messenger.' I'm here to help you through the mediation process; I need your help and the help of your counsel in separating your present value of this dispute from the likely value it would have in court.

"We will consider together the strengths, weaknesses, risks and future expenses of your case—your best 'hoped for' outcome and your worst feared possibility.

"Before we begin, let me ask how each of you want to be addressed? . . . So let's begin with the plaintiff, with permission of course from the plaintiff's attorney. I thank you for choosing mediation and for asking me to assist you."[5]

HELP THE PARTIES CLEAR THEIR LENSES[6]

Rarely do people with strong emotions see the benefit of rational decision-making. Instead, they use raw intuition. They don't do what seems to make sense; they think that things that are more familiar are more frequent. Often the less knowledge they have the more confident they are. They take one piece of information but ignore the base information. It is important, therefore, that mediators find creative ways to help the parties clear their lenses to see more clearly.

Distinguishing between Positions and Interests

Bargaining positions may be expressions of hurt, anger, or a desire to punish, as well as hopes for concessions. Usually parties cannot settle a dispute without modifying either the form or content of their original demands. The mediator helps them distinguish their true underlying needs—those things that must take place for the dispute to be settled—from their original desires, and modify their bargaining positions accordingly.

The mediator is not always passive. Indeed, as the session progresses, the mediator becomes more involved and, at some point, may even have to propose options to the parties by suggesting ideas as a way of helping the parties resolve their own dispute. Making suggestions is one of the mediator's most crucial roles. As an agreement nears, the mediator, as an agent of reality, increases both parties' awareness of the other's needs and builds a realistic framework within which both parties can assess the costs and benefits of continuing or resolving the conflict. One of the most effective approaches in learning about the other's interest is using the mediation approach embodied in the open-ended question, which we will discuss in more detail later in this component. The underlying insight in this approach was described best by Kahlil Gibran: "If he is indeed wise he does not bid you enter the house of his wisdom, but rather leads you to the threshold of your own mind."[7]

Recognizing Benchmarks

Parties start with their own expectations and a benchmark. If they do not reach this benchmark, they perceive this as a loss, a failure. This feeling in turn leads to taking additional risk to avoid more failure. Effective mediation, therefore, involves not crow-barring people down but adjusting their benchmarks. Mediators create options to move benchmarks. The key to moving benchmarks is for the mediator to go beneath the water line with each party—to go beyond stated positions to uncover the real interests, needs, and solutions lying beneath the surface. The mediator needs to take a mental picture in the mind's eye of the following drawing and remember PINS:

PINS

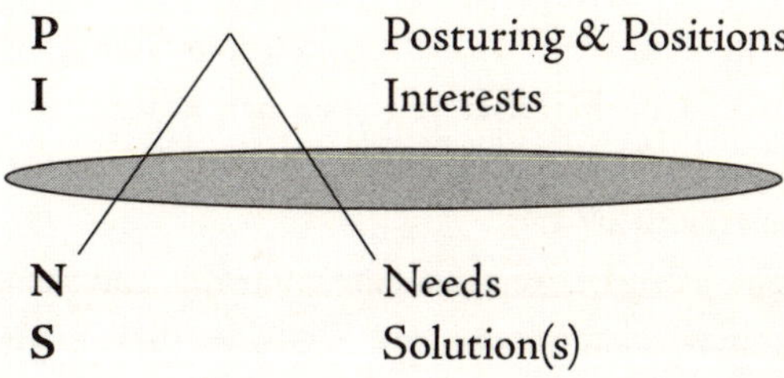

The most effective tool is the question. Use it to probe the posturing of positions above the surface in order to discover below the surface the true interests and needs. The question should be neutral, eliciting information, "When you say you need X, what does it do for you?" (always non-confronting). Use the question to frame an issue. Plant seeds for harvesting later, and allow time for the seeds to grow. Patience is a mediator's best friend. The question is the mediator's next best friend. Mediation is a process that takes time. Use it as stairs to persuade, step by step.

Taking One Bite at a Time

The mediator gives people information on which they make decisions. Anything that is arbitrary is questionable, and naked numbers will clash with each other. Remember that it is the parties that settle cases, not the mediator. People never do things for the mediator's reasons; they do it because it fits into their own agenda.

Reframe, repackage, or restate by saying, "Let me be sure I understand your argument." Then restate their argument as accurately as possible. Use ocean words such as, "to be made whole," "to do the fair thing." In asking questions, the purpose is to receive information that the person wants to give; any answer is okay, so do not interrupt, and be careful not to cross-examine. Be sensitive and step out of the room to allow the parties to talk privately among themselves and with their own counsel.

Practical Tips

Create options and choices by using information, but remain neutral by not giving an opinion. Instead, ask, "I can't answer, but what would you do if a jury decides this issue this way?"

Ask issue questions, not fact questions, without assuming a cross-examination approach. Discuss issues before numbers unless no choice is given. Use open-ended questions: "What is your thinking on the question?"

Use role reversal—ask questions in a particular role and then ask the parties how they feel about the case. Consider picking up in the next question the last word or phrase used in the previous answer. At the end of every answer consider pausing and asking, "What else?"

When asking questions, use twelve words or fewer. To convey a sense of urgency, either lean closer to the parties or remain standing when entering the room.

In presenting a difficult offer, preface it: "I'm afraid you might react negatively to their offer, but here it is." Don't give reasons for the offer, just deliver it. Remember that the other parties will not accept the logic for the offer.

The Open-Ended Question

Some courses of study help us learn facts; learning mediation principles changes our behavior. People want to know how much we care before they care how much we know. Mediation is not subject-matter driven but process driven. People tend to live in two truths. The first truth is what a person says or wants another person to hear—surface structure. The second truth is what a person needs to know—a deeper structure. It is important to live in the open-ended question in order to move from the first truth to the second truth.

Consider prefacing a question with "I wonder," "I'm curious," or "I wonder why." Avoid the use of adjectives or adverbs. In asking questions, be sure to use all three communication techniques: auditory, visual, and kinesthetic. How we ask the question often determines the answer. Use questions beginning with how, when, where, what, why, and what else. This questioning approach should not be to find something wrong or to give advice but rather to help the person achieve an outcome. Don't say, "Do you have any questions?" but rather, "What questions do you have?"

Consider what we want the other to

- See and picture in their minds
- Hear and say to him or herself
- Feel
- Do

Do not make assumptions. Instead, ask for explanations. Take the statement, "Jim is quick." Instead of asking, "What facts do you have?" ask, "What do you mean by quick?" In this process, there are no misunderstandings. Rather there are only *missed* understandings.[8]

> ***Insights from a Fresh Perspective:*** *One great tip I learned in a class called "Communicating with Tact and Finesse" was the use of the phrase "That is interesting; tell me more." When you are not sure you fully understand what the other person is saying or you really want to get the emotions or state of mind, you can use this phrase. This phrase is also a great way to keep the person engaged while you formulate the correct response. Simply saying, "That is interesting" is a good tactic to avoid questions you don't want to answer at that time. It is also a great segue statement to change the subject or move the discussion in a different direction.*

Using the open-ended question is a most effective communication skill. We use it to explore without declaring, to listen without deciding, and to consider alternatives without committing. This technique is perhaps the most important reason for mediation being so successful. It is also a very effective way, in both mediation and negotiation, to send signals without being too explicit.

Focusing on a Settlement Event

Scheduling mediation with the parties' consenting to be present and participate is, by itself, a powerful tactic. It provides a focus on the dispute by all key players; a mutual recognition that this is the appropriate time to offer compromises; and a sense of closure that forces parties to give up illusions. Mediation is often suggested for the primary purpose of getting the other side (for example, an insurance adjuster, plaintiff's counsel, or defense attorney with a large caseload) to focus on this particular dispute. The fact that all sides have agreed to mediate sends a mutual signal that everyone has recognized the need to compromise. The time limits inherent in the mediation process create a settlement event. Properly nurtured, mediation has a train-is-leaving-the-station quality that forces parties to face illusions of victory and the risks, embarrassments, and frustrations often inherent in settling. The settlement event is a psychological condition, which is effective only to the degree that it exists in the participants' minds.[9]

Harnessing Existing Passion

One of the greatest assets available to the mediator is the seething passion among the parties. This passion, when lifted out of the chaos, transplanted, and successfully harnessed, fuels the dynamism that motivates the parties to start building anew. Most parties enter into negotiations certain of their cause but uncertain of their ability to negotiate a successful conclusion; thus, at the outset of a mediation, the certainty-uncertainty dynamic is pointed in favor of the pre-existing configuration that has led to stagnation, impasse, and conflict. In a more productive, dynamic mediation, parties become certain that their legitimate interests will be satisfied to the greatest extent possible but uncertain as to how. Passion can be a positive magnetic force. When trying to bring together positive forces, as when holding the like poles of magnets together, they repel. The mediator works to identify these conflicting passions, normalize their existence, and then harness this passionate energy toward a productive conclusion.[10]

COMBINE NEGOTIATION SKILLS

Our focus in Part II, "Becoming More Skilled," has been on listening actively, using sound strategies and tactics, and adopting principles of mediation as additional negotiation tactics. Remember that mediation does not attempt to change the other's position. Instead it encourages us to be patient and allow enough time for the process to work, to use open-ended questions, and to probe beneath the surface of ideas exchanged to decipher interests and needs.

Now it is time for us to combine our various negotiating skills into a whole. In this concluding part, we will move from a focus on Becoming More Skilled to a focus on Being More Persuasive. We will consider the subtlety of signals, the art of persuasion, and the effectiveness of affirming timeless values. The message in the title of this book serves as a review summary of our continued focus on the dynamic tension that exists between the competitive force of the negotiator mind-set and the ethical force of timeless values: *Deal Makers: Negotiating More Effectively Using Timeless Values.*

What patterns in mediation are similar to those in negotiation?

Summary

- Assume the mediator role and mediate your own negotiation.
- Be patient and allow time for the mediation process to work.
- Use open-ended questions.
- Respect feelings, even if those feelings are illogical.
- Go beneath the surface and change the benchmarks by changing interests, needs, and solutions instead of attempting to change a person's position.
- Create a settlement event.
- Harness existing passions.
- Apply Mediation Principles

NOTES

1. William Ury, *Getting Past No, Negotiating With Difficult People,* Rev. Ed. (New York: Bantam Books, 1993), 109.
2. This paragraph adopted from, John Leo Wagner, "Aggressive ADR?" in *Business Law Today* (May/June 1999).
3. Ideas for this section adopted from seminar presented by Mediation & Arbitration Professional Systems, Inc. (MAPS), New Orleans, Louisiana.
4. Ibid.

5. Ibid.
6. This section adopted from Harvey Sector, Dean of The Law School in Winnipeg, Canada, speaking at the Advanced Mediator Training seminar at MAPS in New Orleans.
7. Kahlil Gibran, *The Prophet,* (Wordsworth Classics of World Literature, 1997), 34.
8. Ideas for this section adapted from presentation made by Richard Lucas, Ph.D., at seminar by Attorneys-Mediators Institute, Dallas, Texas.
9. Ibid.
10. See Suzan L. Podziba's article in *Negotiation Journal* (October 2003), 285, 288. Podziba is a public policy mediator who previously taught at MIT and Harvard.

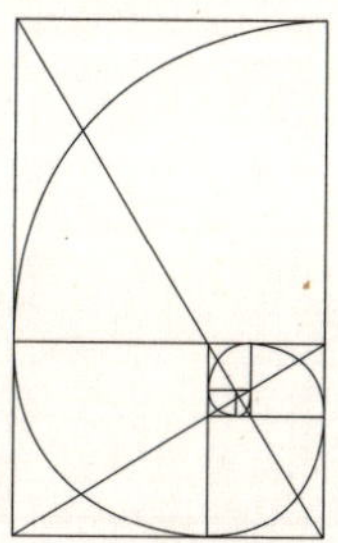

Part III: Being More Persuasive

Component Eight:

Communicate through Signals

Tuning into the Non-verbal Approach

As we move from a focus on the separate skills needed as a negotiator to a focus on being more persuasive, we learn how to combine our skills into a unified approach and how to maintain flexibility by communicating through the subtlety of signals. These signals often convey more meaning than words. And they can be clarified when needed without appearing contradictory.

The overwhelming majority of all communication is non-verbal. Effective persuasion founded on trust, therefore, depends more on showing rather than telling. Reputation for trust precedes the negotiator with amazing speed. And what is also interesting is that it is often conveyed, non-verbally, through subtle signals. This trust in another is sensed, rather than reached as a result of systematic reasoning. At a particular moment, we just "know" when we can trust that person. This intuitive judgment later may be proven wrong, but this doesn't deter us from continuing to use the subtlety of signals.

Being persuasive requires a capacity for compassion and care in order to empathize with the other. This is accomplished through human interaction and through the ability "to sit in a negotiation and figure out the subtext of the discussion that's coursing beneath the explicit words."[1] Empathy is largely about emotion—about feeling what another is feeling. "Just as the mode of the rational mind is words, the mode of the emotions is nonverbal."[2]

SET THE TONE

The first two or three minutes of negotiating sets the tone and gives initial clues to the other side not only about where we as negotiators plan to go but also the way in which we plan to get there. We must watch for signals of emotional distance needed by an opponent and perceive when we are being warned not to overstep the other's personal boundaries.[3] We listen intently to the nuances in words, particularly those which are very carefully drafted.

Creating a Constructive Presence

Empathizing is very different from systematizing, where a certain degree of detachment is needed. Empathizing, in contrast, requires "some degree of attachment in order to recognize that you are interacting with a person, not an object, but a person with feelings, and whose feelings affect your own."[4]

> ***Insights from a Fresh Perspective:*** *I am reminded of two mechanics I used to work with as an engineer. Bob was clueless as a mechanic, but he was always well-dressed, well-groomed, and displayed a big smile. He could look people right in the eyes and tell them the most awful bunch of nonsense they ever heard. Joe, on the other hand, was an excellent mechanic. He really understood machinery, but Joe wasn't much to look at. His clothes were often rumpled, and he wasn't very clean most of the time. He would never look a person in the face; he always looked down and mumbled. The main difference that struck me about these two was the way they used nonverbal communication. Clueless Bob made excellent use of nonverbal signals, causing everyone to think he actually knew what he was doing. But the true expert, Joe, lacked all credibility, even when he was right time after time, because he lacked nonverbal communication skills.*

A law student at the University of Tennessee made a class presentation with such a powerful constructive presence that I asked him where he had studied acting. He answered, "I've never done acting. I was a police officer." I asked him to write about his experience.

> "Constructive force refers to the impression that physical

presence and demeanor convey. This demeanor is part of police officers' training. In that arena, constructive force is the lowest form of force and first communicates the message that its proponent means business.

The elements of constructive force are bearing or demeanor, dress, physical stance and signals, voice control and word choice, and anything else that one can think of that announces: this is who I am, this is how I carry myself, and this is how I conduct my business. These intangibles are construed as force because they provide our opponent an insight into our professionalism, preparation, confidence and resolve.

What precisely comprises constructive force? How you dress—are you wearing a jacket and tie or golf shirt and jeans? Is your attire neat, pressed, and laundered? Buttoned? How do you carry files and documents—loose and messy or organized within a brief case or file box? How do you stand and speak when addressing an opponent or the court? Are you slouching? Do you appear to be in control? Is your demeanor meek or overbearing? Do you project your voice and remain professional? The list can continue with many combinations. The key is this: the more put-together you present yourself, the more put-together and forceful you will appear. This leads to people taking you seriously, buying into your confidence, and at least thinking twice before challenging you. In a dispute this can mean time saved negotiating petty points or initial positions, or better, an opponent being less likely to take risks or force our hand. In law enforcement, a good showing of constructive force can mean the difference between a peaceful resolution and a violent or deadly encounter."[5]

Looking for the Silent Message

Let the soul's ear tell us what it hears and then trust it. This is not mystical. This is merely giving full faith and credit, as it were, to the vast storehouse of knowledge an individual gathers. As we proceed through life, the reservoir of knowledge fills—gradually, steadily, imperceptibly. Words are chosen, usually unconsciously. How they come together—the syntax, tone, inflection—often carries more information about what is being said and who is saying it than the individual words themselves. We have the ability to call instantly upon the mind's reservoir to sort through the billions of items of information stored there to select what is relevant. People who listen to the disclosures of their soul's ear are said to be intuitive. All people possess the soul's ear, and it will report to us if we only listen.[6]

> ***Insights from a Fresh Perspective:*** *I walked into the meeting confident, prepared and ready to protect my job. The head of personnel was sitting sideways in his chair with his arm across the back of the chair next to him, while the principal was looking down at some papers and fidgeting with a folder. I sat across the table from them. I sat up straight in my chair and looked each one of them in the eye. The principal started with a shoot-the-breeze type of question. I answered, looking him straight in the eye. Then they started in with the evaluation. While the principal was speaking to me, he would not look me in the eyes, he shuffled papers, clicked his pen, and deferred each question I had to the personnel director. I remained straight in my chair, and when it was my turn to speak, I leaned in slightly while presenting my data and statistics. The head of personnel shifted, removing his arm from the back of the chair next to him and began to straighten up in his chair, while the principal continued to shuffle papers. I knew their intentions as well as my own and tried to understand both sides. This hour-long meeting lasted for thirteen minutes; I walked away with my job and the schedule that I wanted for next year.*

Tuning into the Clues

Most people seem to believe that there is nothing more to communication than listening to another person's speech and observing their outward movements. In other words, they think that they can rely implicitly on another person's visible signals to convey a correct picture of invisible thoughts, feelings, and intentions. The matter is not as simple as this. As all traditional teachings point out, "We can understand other beings only to the extent that we know ourselves." Naturally, close observation and careful listening are necessary. But even perfect observation and perfect listening lead to nothing unless the information obtained is correctly interpreted and understood. The precondition to our ability to understand correctly is our own self-knowledge—our own inner experience.[7]

When I was buying an old plantation home in a rural area some thirty-five miles north of my home in the city, I remember sitting in a back room office of a country lawyer who was representing me in the transaction. Just before leaving, I stood at the door and asked, "Bob, you know, I may end up moving up here someday. What kind of people would be my neighbors?"

"Bill, sit down." Bob then proceeded to tell me about a traveler who asked two travelers approaching him.

"'What kind of people live in yonder town?'

"The quick reply was, 'Well, what kind of people lived in your town?'

"'What does that have to do with it?'

"'Everything,' explained the approaching travelers. 'If in your town there were mainly back-biting contentious people who rarely laughed, you will find them in yonder town—but if in the town from where you came there were fun-loving, happy people you enjoyed being with, then these are the kind of people you will find in yonder town.'"

> ***Insights from a Fresh Perspective:*** *In the September 8, 1997 issue of the* New Yorker, *there is a non-fiction account by an oncologist about the death of one of his patients, a 54-year-old Wall Street tycoon. The story is titled "The Last Deal." The doctor's initial evaluation contains the following: "As he spoke, Kirk Bains locked his jaundiced eyes on mine. He was obviously studying my face, looking for clues, trying to read my response in advance. I imagined it was a style he adopted in his business meetings where he would face down clients by looking hard into their eyes, to gauge whether the project and the people before him were worth his resources. This time though the roles were reversed." So far, I have been only slightly tuned into the clues people give with body language. I look at them when they speak but I am not reading them consciously. I have always been a hunter and fisherman and have developed good "sign reading skills" for those field sports. Not thinking of people as quarry, I never realized I had the need for these same skills in the arena of human relations. This is what negotiation asks me to do.*

Recognizing the Signal Sent

In January 1950, Secretary of State Dean Acheson made a widely quoted speech before the National Press Club. He declared, "America's line of defense runs along the Aleutians to Japan and then goes to the Ryukyu Islands . . . the defense perimeter runs from the Ryukus to the Philippine Islands." He thus drew a line on a map in which Korea was demarcated as being outside the area we would defend, a clear signal to the North Koreans. On June 24, 1950, the Korean War broke out when North Korea invaded South Korea. To the end of his life, Acheson vigorously denied that he had given the green light for aggression in South Korea by excluding it from the perimeter.[8]

LISTEN FOR THE PAUSE

Using Rhythm[9]

What happens when two people talk? That is really the basic question here because that's the basic context in which all persuasion takes place. People talk back and forth. They listen. They interrupt. They move their hands. Their conversation has a rhythmic physical dimension. Research shows that each person (within a fraction of a second) moves a shoulder or cheek or eyebrow or a hand, sustains that movement, and starts again. These movements are in time to each person's own words so that the speakers are, in effect, dancing to their own speech. At the same time, the other people around the table are dancing along, moving their faces, shoulders, hands, and bodies in the same rhythm. It's not that everyone is moving the same way, it's that the timing of the stops and starts of each person's micro-movements—the shifts of the body and face—are perfectly in harmony.

Subsequent research has revealed that when two people talk, their volume and pitch fall into balance. Speech rate—the number of speech sounds per second—equalizes. So does the period of time lapses between the moment one speaker stops talking and the moment the other speaker begins. And, like all specialized human traits, some people have much more mastery over this reflex than others. Part of what it means to have a powerful or persuasive personality, then, is that we can draw others into our own rhythms.

Practical Tips

When the other person responds with "maybe," "I guess so," or "is that right?" there could be hidden opposition.

When a person prefaces a statement with: "to tell the truth," "honestly," "frankly," or, "I'm laying all my cards on the table," chances are that the person is being neither honest nor frank.

Some people tend to compromise when they are tired or when the other has been persistent; others become antagonistic.

Frequency of leg movements, degree of eye contact, taking glasses off, and fidgeting with objects such as a pen or pencil may give clues of a person being deceptive or evasive.

Frequency of throat-clearing and touch of mouth or face with hands indicate anxiety, discomfort, or serious evaluation.

Arm crossed on the chest (like an umpire in a baseball game) may indicate defensiveness.

When a person says, "It isn't the money, it's the principle of the thing," chances are it's the money.

Tension is often shown by dilation of the pupils, visible perspiration, or rising voice level.

Increasing distance between the parties indicates growing distrust.

A well-organized file may indicate a readiness to reach agreement.

> ***Insights from a Fresh Perspective:*** *Compare negotiating silence to a pause in music. A pause is not a lack of music. It is an integral part of the composition. As Claude Debussy has said, "Music is the space between the notes." If a conductor does not hold a pause for its full value, it is like cutting into the flesh of the music. While remaining silent, the astute negotiator may assess the bargaining power of his adversary through the adversary's words and actions, and then execute his own game plan.*

Accepting the Subtlety of Signals

Each move is at the same time both a position of substance and a Pavlovian signal to the other party to stop or continue in the direction already taken. This is particularly true when the size of each concession signals what's to come. If each of the other's concessions is progressively smaller, even if the other continues to say, "I want to settle this," the message is that a final offer is approaching. So be on the lookout for non-verbal communication that is inconsistent with the spoken word because what a person is and what a person does speaks much louder than what a person says. "Be careful not to telegraph to the other side your need to settle. . . . Go to school on the other party, on what you think they think your position is."[10]

> ***Insights from a Fresh Perspective:*** *Any classical dance is a depiction of a theme and the dancer is the storyteller. In the Indian dance "Bharatnatyam," the dancer performs with Bhavas and Rasas. Bhavas are the imitations of emotions that the actors perform, and Rasas are the emotional responses that the audience experiences. In real life we also have involuntary expressions that convey emotions. In my opinion, the expression of the eye is the strongest weapon. It conveys more than words and other expressions. If we know how to use this powerfully, we can make our way through to even the strongest of minds.*

MAINTAIN EMOTIONAL CONTROL

We should use emotions to give us the edge "but avoid fear and greed."[11] It seems likely that evolutionary dynamics have developed negative emotions (fear and anger) to engage more quickly and with greater force than positive emotions (joy and serenity) because the former carry greater survival potential. Readiness and strength are more likely to save a person at critical moments than are contentment and trust. Evolution rewards that which works best, not that which feels best. Undoubtedly, the two most intense emotions that confront negotiators are fear and anger. Anger can flash white-hot at a moment's notice, and fear can reduce the negotiator to paralysis. Fear in negotiations arises in a variety of circumstances. If a negotiator faces an aggressive opponent, bargains without adequate preparation, senses that an opponent has superior bargaining power, or feels insecure about ability, it is normal to experience moderate to extreme levels of fear.[12]

In controlling emotions, think about meta-emotions (the emotion a person has about emotions) because the meta-emotion often influences the primary emotion being experienced. For example, "I may be happy, ashamed, or angry about being angry."[13]

Practical Tips

If someone asks a direct question like, "What is your profit potential?" You answer indirectly: "Well, in the past five years, profits have increased 15 percent each year"—and be silent.

Dress and appearance (from a female general counsel): "Looks do matter—be professional in appearance; you don't want to look like a man, a little girl, one of the guys, or your mother."[14]

Put off using words. Send nonverbal signals; verbal responses are not always required. It is estimated that 70 to 80 percent of what we learn about others is through non-verbal signals.[15]

Release additional information gradually, and control the flow. To avoid discussing a topic prematurely, say, "Let's come back to that." Leave some silent space for emphasis.

Tell a story about a similar situation as a pause in the negotiations.[16]

Watch for changes in facial expressions, eye contact, and spatial conversation distance. Voice tone with rising intonation elicits a response; falling intonation signals routine message. Watch your television interviewer.

Voice inflection is critical:

- WHY do you say that?
- Why do YOU say that?
- Why do you say THAT?

Insights from a Fresh Perspective: *"Kathak" is a North Indian dance where the dancer tells a story through her movements, expression, and the footwork/rhythm. Usually, words are not used to express any emotion throughout the performance. The "real audience" must be able to relate to this experience without the aid of speech. The dancer's movement, speed, poise and grace, facial expressions, aligned hand gestures and expression of music, need to be all tied together to actually get the message across. It can be*

> *a folk tale or it can be describing the space of the feelings of lover or mother, but they are all understood without any use of words. Every person in the audience would relate to this story in the way they perceive this interactive expression from the performer and the music, based on how they value each of the emotions in their personal lives. A negotiator will also have to understand what is said, what is between the words, and feelings of the opponent, to truly get the gist of the message.*

Determining When and How to Present Numbers

Presenting numbers in a negotiation deserves special attention. Psychological research shows there is a certain capacity, limit, or amount of space in our brain for certain kinds of information. How many variables can we focus on at the same time? Listening to five high-pitched tones, we would be able to tell them apart; five low-pitched tones, we would be able to tell them apart. We would think, then, that if those high and low tones were combined, and were played all at once, we would be able to divide them into ten categories. Chances are, however, we would still be stuck at about six categories.[17]

In commercial transactions, it is often helpful to summarize on one sheet of paper not more than five numerical variables that are critical to the deal. More criteria are not always better. The process of arriving at these five variables alone can be very rewarding. A negotiation based largely on numerical reasoning should be aimed at the numbers-driven financial manager on the opposing team.[18]

Consider using precise—not rounded—numbers. Try to think less in black and white and more in terms of the big picture, the circumstances surrounding, and the reasons for the numbers. "Focus not just on the numbers, which are merely symbols, but on the message behind the numbers in order to give meaning to the numbers. . . . Each situation is a unique situation. The person who can add value and give meaning to the numbers is needed. If we don't do this we are not adding value."[19]

"As an engineer, I always thought it's black or white. Then I found out in the area of mergers and acquisitions, there is no black or white, only shades of grey. I always tell my client this will work because we reach an area of commercial reasonableness . . . start the deal generally . . . don't trip over the details . . . arrange a general agreement that can be set on a single sheet of paper with plenty of white . . . save the details for later . . ."[20]

Let your numbers tell a story gradually. And be sure to listen carefully for non-verbal signals before continuing with an additional idea.

Using Questions to Control

Use questions to uncover patterns. Negotiators are like fingerprints: no two are alike—but that doesn't mean they don't have some similarities or that there are no common patterns present. Don't just try one technique after another, like pulling arrows out of a quiver and shooting until one hits something. Instead, use questions to control negotiations and to see the other party's motives, fears, and desires.[21]

> ***Insights from a Fresh Perspective:*** *Forty thousand fans rise to their feet. The game is tied, 2–2, bottom of the ninth. You glance at the scoreboard, one out, one ball, and two strikes. You turn around to the runner on second; allow a base hit and you lose the game. Your heart thumps with adrenaline as you take the sign from the catcher. A slow curve falls into the catcher's mitt, a foot outside the strike zone; ball two. You follow the same routine; glance at the scoreboard, turn around to the runner on second, and rifle a ninety-five mile per hour fastball high and tight; a swing and a miss. Strike three, two outs. In baseball, like negotiations, you often give ground to set your opponent up for your next move. Two outs, bottom of the ninth, with the home team's last chance at the plate. You glance at the scoreboard, check the runner on second and unleash a low change-up, already knowing your next pitch.*

Seeing Things in a Different Way

Perceptions, not objective reality, are the driving force behind negotiations because ultimately it is the reality as each side sees it that constitutes the problem in a negotiation and opens the way to a solution.[22]

Try to see with the "mind's eye," to imagine how the pattern of a negotiation is unfolding. Even though we use the template of these patterns as a starting map, the reality of the situation (the hidden forces, tensions, and agendas) often do not agree with what we first thought. Consider using a sketch, charts, or drawings to signal a pattern and tell the story we want to tell. When the brain is weary of its verbal chatter, making a drawing or graph is a way to increase perception of how we see things and how we feel. In a sense, we have shifted to a new mode of seeing. We take new approaches to problems, correct old misperceptions, and peel away layers of stereotypes that keep us from clear seeing.[23]

A helpful exercise for seeing things in a different way is the decision-tree approach used in game theory as developed by John Nash. Each major branch on the tree depicts a particular alternative, followed by smaller branches showing possible consequences of that decision. As considered in Component Five, it is important to complete the tree and hold back reaching any conclusion (which tends to close down thinking about other alternatives). Then look at the process backwards, starting with the smaller branches of consequences and move inward toward the decision nodes. "Be imaginative to think about solving even those problems that haven't come up yet . . . use your ability to think beyond the problem in front of you . . . strike when the iron is hot and recognize the opportunity to settle and the reality of your situation."[24]

Two people can see the same thing, disagree, and yet both be right. It is not logical; it's psychological. We don't need the facts to have an opinion, for we do not see the lens through which we look.[25] We tend to see ourselves primarily in the light of our intentions, which are invisible to others. Meanwhile, we see others mainly in the light of their actions, which are visible, so we have a situation in which misunderstanding is the order of the day.[26] We may not always be what we appear to be, but what we appear to be is always a significant part of what we are. These signals we send to other people within seven seconds of first meeting them often reveal our hidden agenda because we ourselves are the message.[27]

> ***Insights from a Fresh Perspective:*** *Above all, be in control during the negotiation process, no matter what happens, because the other side will be watching. Lieutenant Daniel Kaffee, in the movie* A

> Few Good Men, *summed it up best: "So remember, don't flinch when something doesn't go your way, don't hang your head, don't shift in your seat, don't scribble furiously, whatever happens you have to look like it's exactly what you knew was going to happen."*

Accepting Deadlines as Added Leverage

A timeline with an impending deadline is one of the most powerful forces in negotiations. It sends a signal that the force of time and the expectation of a beneficial outcome are in tension. If the negotiation is not time-critical, consider trying to reach a mutual agreement to establish an artificial deadline.[28]

Using Constructive Ambiguity

Use "constructive ambiguity" if agreement on all details is not possible.[29] By avoiding discussion of specifics, we send a signal that a general agreement can be reached. When a detail of our position is attacked, as in wrestling, avoid putting all our strength directly against our opponent. Instead, step aside and ask questions to channel energy toward different options and toward exploring the other's interests. See the opponent's attack as being on the problem, not on us as individuals, and try to solve the problem with more general solutions.

Clarity and precision in communicating are often good, but there is a time and place for ambiguity. Signals are useful in negotiations precisely because they are subtle, flexible, not completely clear, and therefore, disavowable. They hint, point, imply, or suggest—and if ambiguous enough, they can easily be clarified so as not to deny previous statements. Ambiguous statements can also be used to keep talks going simply because further clarification is needed. In addition, ambiguous demands make face-saving concessions easier because clarifying an imprecise statement is usually better than having to equivocate after making one that is too precise.[30]

We are now ready to continue exploring subtleties in negotiating communication as we review the classical art of persuasion in our next component.

What patterns do you recognize when communicating through signals?

Summary

- Be aware of your facial expressions, especially when you are listening.
- Adjust the tempo of your speech to match the opponent's tempo.
- Look for the opponent's hidden message.
- Put off using words; instead use signals.
- Respect the other's space.
- Give the explanation before presenting the numbers.
- Adopt a deadline for added leverage.

NOTES

1. Daniel H. Pink, *A Whole New Mind, Why Right-Brainers Will Rule the Future* (NY: The Penguin Group, 2006), 163.
2. Ibid., 162. Often the most determining nonverbal messages are sent in the first seven seconds. Roger Ailes, *You Are the Message* (N.I. Doubleday, 1995), 3.
3. Roger Fisher and Daniel Shapiro, *Beyond Reason: Using Emotions As You Negotiate* (New York: Viking, 2005), 64.
4. Pink, *A Whole New Mind*, 173.
5. Student, University of Tennessee College of Law, 2004, speaking to the class.
6. Gerry Spence, *ABA Journal* (January 1995). See also, Gerry Spence, *How to Argue and Win Every Time*, (New York, St. Martins, 1995), 70.
7. E.F. Schumacher, *A Guide for the Perplexed* (New York: Harper Perennial, 1978), 84.
8. William Manchester, *American Caesar: Douglas MacArthur 1880–1964* (New York: Dell, 1983), 541.
9. Malcolm Gladwell, *The Tipping Point: How Little Things Can Make a Big Difference* (Boston: Little, Brown and Company, 2000), 82–83.

10. Ben L. Day, Attorney, Baton Rouge, speaking to the class.
11. Laurence Tisch, advisor in securities investing, "Corporate Shoot-Out at Black Rock" *Time* (September 22, 1986).
12. Adler, Rosen, and Silverstein, "Emotions in Negotiation," *Negotiation Journal* 14 (April 1998), 161, 174.
13. Adopted from article by Tricia S. Jones and Andrea Bodtker in *Negotiation Journal* 17 (July 2001), 207, 239.
14. Mary Beth Arceneaux, General Counsel for Louisiana Bankers Association, speaking to the class.
15. Albert Mehrabian, *Silent Messages: Implicit Communication of Emotions and Attitudes* (Wadsworth Publishing Company, 1980), 8–39.
16. Charlie Phillips, former senior partner of Taylor, Porter, Brooks & Phillips, Baton Rouge, Louisiana.
17. Gladwell, *The Tipping Point*, 175.
18. D.B.H. Chaffe, III, Chaffe & Associates, New Orleans, speaking to the class.
19. David Broussard, CPA, Baton Rouge, speaking to the class.
20. D.B.H. Chaffe, III, Chaffe & Associates, New Orleans, speaking to the class.
21. Adopted from John Patrick Doland, in tape series "Negotiate Like the Pros."
22. John S. Murray, Alan Scott Rau, and Edward F. Sherman, *Negotiation* (Foundation Press, 1996), 73, 163.
23. Betty Edwards, *Drawing on the Right Side of the Brain*, Rev. Ed. (New York: Tarcher/Penguin USA, 1989), 21–24.
24. Mary Olive Pierson, attorney, Baton Rouge, speaking to the class.
25. Stephen R. Covey, *Seven Habits of Highly Effective People: Powerful Lessons in Personal Change* (Free Press, 1989), 30–32, 41–42, 67.
26. E.F. Schumacher, *A Guide for the Perplexed* (New York: Harper Perennial, 1978), 84.
27. Roger Ailes, *You Are the Message* (Doubleday, 1988), 3.
28. Henry S. Kramer, *Game, Set, Match: Winning the Negotiation Game* (ALM Publishing/ALM Inc., 2001), 323.

29. "An Interview with Kissinger," *Time* (August 13, 1979), http://www.time.com/time/magazine/article/0,9171,919998,00.html.
30. David Churchman, *Negotiation: Process, Tactics, Theory* (Lanham MD, University Press of America, 1995), 48–49.

Component Nine:

Adopt the Art of Persuasion

Preserving Relationships

We experience something unique as we improve our idea-having and problem-solving abilities and as we improve our ability to listen and communicate clearly. We begin to feel the power of artistic creativity. We see our negotiation skills combined into an art form, the art of persuasion. Like other art forms, this art involves both a *moment* in time, as does a great painting, and a *movement* in time, as does an inspiring piece of music. Planning our strategy and using our communication skills is akin to that exhibited by both the painter and the musician. Both use a similar story-telling technique, but in negotiations, we must be careful to depend on the facts of the story and a careful organization rather than on judgments and opinions. This allows us to use the art of persuasion by showing, rather than by telling.

MOVE OUR FOCUS TO THE WHOLE

When an idea or focus moves from an invention to an innovation, we must look at the "big picture" where the parts come together. In this component, we direct our attention not to a particular negotiating skill, but to a combination of skills in the overall art of persuasion. We move our focus to the larger picture and try to see reality objectively.

Most of us have been taught at one time or another to break apart problems in order to make complex tasks more manageable. But if we are not careful, we may pay an enormous price for simply fragmenting every problem in order to find the best solution. If we focus only on the individual pieces, we may not be able to reassemble, list, and organize all the components. We may find the task similar to trying to reassemble the fragments of a broken mirror in order to see a true reflection of the whole.

Daniel H. Pink, in his mind-stretching book *A Whole New Mind: Why Right-Brainers Will Rule the Future*, explains that there are two fundamental ways of interpreting information: breaking the whole into its components, or weaving the components into a whole.[1] He then shows how the left hemisphere of our brains analyzes the details of information; how the right hemisphere synthesizes the big picture. What we need today is not the ability to grasp details but the ability to reorganize patterns, to interpret emotions and nonverbal expressions, to build relationships, to see the big picture, and to engage in complex synthesis. Therefore, we must focus on our ability "to create artistic and emotional beauty, which uses more holistic, intuitive, and nonlinear reasoning."[2]

Our mental models are often deeply ingrained assumptions, generalizations, or images that influence how we make decisions. We are often unaware of our mental models or the effects they have on our negotiation decisions. It is hard to think of new, innovative negotiation techniques when we are bound tightly by our mental model. This prevents us from gaining new insights. But just being aware of these built-in restrictions on our thinking is half the battle. Discipline is needed to turn the mirror inward, to unearth our internal picture, to move our inner ideas to the surface, and to hold them rigorously to scrutiny.

Practical Tips

The main approach to persuading is to show, not tell. It is better to use a story-telling technique that depends on facts and careful organization, not judgments and opinions. Try to group the key facts (with the big ideas first) into a series of verbal pictures, word snapshots that persuade by showing.[3]

Show genuine interest by concentrating and listening intently. Always allow emotional dialogue to precede intellectual discussion.[4]

Evaluate after the opponent's idea is complete, not before. Use an opponent's name. Don't listen anxiously or interrupt except to ask for clarification.[5]

ESTABLISH TRUST AT THE BEGINNING

Establishing trust at the beginning of a negotiation builds a relationship, which is critical because it is difficult to negotiate where neither party will trust.[6] Aristotle states, "People believe a good person more fully and more readily than others. Three things inspire confidence in character and induce people to believe a thing apart from the proof of it: good sense, good moral character, and good will."[7]

All of us, no matter our profession, need trust. We have to be able to rely on others acting as they say they will, and we need others to accept that we will act as we say we will.[8]

Thinking with Others

The synergy produced when we share, rather than just negotiate, ideas with others is often remarkable. When we choose to explore new alternatives and postpone making decisions, our chances for an innovative solution increase dramatically. We learn to see gradual processes that require slowing down our rush. These gradual processes often reveal a pattern that provides the needed insight. Sometimes, as pointed out by Malcolm Gladwell, it is the smallest of changes that produces the greatest results.[9]

Developing Relationships

Persuasive skills that are easy to acquire but often overlooked are the developing and preserving of relationships. We treat an opponent with respect, not as an object to be pushed but as a person to be persuaded. An approach that is too direct doesn't work either in courtship or in negotiations.[10]

We should not start a negotiation by saying, "Just give me a number," or, "Give me a price," as is said to the antique dealer in the Arthur Miller play, *The Price*. The story starts with an off-duty policeman looking through the phone book for an antique dealer to whom he can sell his father's old desk, which is in storage, in a building that is about to be torn down. The man chooses the oldest dealership and gives them a ring. The elderly antique dealer says he will be right over. Out of breath after climbing five flights of stairs, the antique dealer knocks on the door of the room where the desk is stored. The door swings open and the policeman says, "Just give me a price." This is the refrain the policeman repeatedly asks in their ensuing conversation. Finally, the antique dealer says, "Look, I'm way older than you are, and if anyone should be in a hurry, it should be me! Not you . . . and, besides, how can I ever give you a price if I don't know you?" By the end of the play, a relationship of trust is established, a price is given, and the old desk is sold.

A winning argument is possible when, speaking out of our personal authority, we address the authority of the other, because the logic of a position will mean nothing to an opponent who doesn't trust us. Fairness is a tiny voice that thunders from behind every argument.[11]

In a feature article published in *USA Today* called "Ready to Start Your Business?", ten questions were asked under the heading, "Do you have the right stuff to start a business?" The eighth question was, "Are you honest, trustworthy, and committed to avoiding evil? In today's world, good first impressions heavily impact the success of a new venture, and even a whiff of dishonesty can spell disaster."[12] Experienced negotiators stress the power of character. In fact, some state that when there is character, negotiation strength is doubled.[13]

> ***Insights from a Fresh Perspective:*** *While discussing reliability, Professors Roger Fisher and Scott Brown point out that both trust and suspicion are just states of mind; they are merely perceptions we hold in our minds of another person. As a result, we trust people sometimes when it is counterproductive to do so. We make decisions about their intentions based on our personal interpretation of the information that is filtered through our lenses. This is where we can go wrong. There should be a more stable reason behind trust or suspicion than just personal perception of a person. Keep in mind the idea of professional trust as risk analysis. A trust based on risk analysis focuses on potential risks involved in relying on them. The best example would be a con artist. A con artist knows exactly what to do in order to earn someone's trust. He is someone who knows and understands a person's lenses and perceptions better than the person does. He can see himself with his victim's eyes and filter his words, mannerisms, and actions through their lenses and see what is expected of him next. Risk analysis would stop him dead in his tracks.*

Using Dialogue Imaginatively

Dialogue, according to Daniel Yankelovich in *The Magic of Dialogue: Transforming Conflict into Cooperation*[14], is a unique form of persuasion because it has capabilities other forms of talk do not possess. It seeks a genuine openness of each party to the concerns of the other. One listens and responds to the other with an authenticity that forges a bond, as distinguished from a negotiating device that seeks to overcome conflict and reach an agreement leading to action. In fact, some of dialogue's most striking successes (for example, in relations with the former Soviet Union) have occurred because dialogue preceded, and was sharply distinguished from, formal negotiations. Dialogue played a special role in reversing the nuclear arms race and ending the Cold War. Some years after the end of Ronald Reagan's presidency, George Schultz, who had been Reagan's Secretary of State, asked Mikhail Gorbachev, former president of the Soviet Union, what the turning point in the Cold War had been. "Reykjavík," Gorbachev answered without hesitation. He explained that at their meeting in Reykjavík, Iceland, he and Ronald Reagan had entered into a genuine dialogue for the first time that extended far beyond their main agenda of arms control to cover their values, assumptions, and aspirations for their respective nations.

Gorbachev credited this dialogue with establishing enough trust and mutual understanding to begin to reverse the nuclear arms race. Once dialogue creates mutual understanding, the climate becomes conducive to decision making. Nothing ruins more promising dialogues and undermines more decisions than the failure to keep the two processes separate.

Practical Tips

Remember that good record keeping adds to your power. No one is smart enough to remember everything one knows. "Always support your position with lots of paper—document everything, use tangible and demonstrable evidence such as pictures and X-Rays."[15]

Staying Goal Focused

In negotiations, set a goal and, as in golf and tennis, develop a momentum that is goal-oriented. Create a range of alternative solutions and be aware of the effect of synergy—the combination of different solutions because certain types of order provide foundations on which to build new structures, including methods of indexing and tracking information.[16]

Strains of stupidity affect the smart, says a Nobel Prize winning astrophysicist. Fanatics get distracted by detail, by complexity, by the esoteric. They dig one hole, boring in, getting more and more fascinated about less and less. Really good ideas ultimately have something simple at the bottom of them. Sometimes it is best to focus and say, this is what I'm not going to work on. This is the opposite of the person fixated on one minor thing.[17]

I'll never forget the day when Mrs. T first came to see me. She sat up straight in the small wooden chair instead of the old, leather, cushioned one and said, "I have a problem. I'm single, with three grown children, and due to retire in three months. And I'm not going to receive any social security because I first worked for the state and they have a separate retirement system. . . . And I'm not covered by the state retirement system because of some rule change. Can you help me?"

A review of the facts showed that, indeed, Mrs. T was not entitled to any retirement benefits. In our next conferences, I asked her to stay focused and help me review carefully all of her assets. She said that she didn't have any except for a narrow strip of sugar cane land between Baton Rouge and New Orleans on the Mississippi River. The front portion was leased to a farmer for a few hundred dollars a year. The rear portion was in the swamp. A quick check of the records revealed that her property was located on the deep channel side of the river, very suitable for barge anchoring. In addition, some new industrial plants had moved into the area. A commercial realtor contact mentioned that this particular bend of the river was a prime industrial site. I checked further and found that Mrs. T's strip of land lay right between two larger tracts, neither of which was large enough by itself to satisfy industrial requirements.

I examined her title and compared it with surveys of the property.

Everything checked out. So I notified the realtor that my client had clear title verified by existing surveys. I cautioned Mrs. T not to discuss the matter with anyone without calling me first, to stay focused on one goal, and to be patient. A month later, we were in serious negotiations for the sale of her property at a premium price, a sale that we insisted would include not just the frontage the buyer wanted, but her entire tract, stretching back in the swamp some forty arpents, or about 7,700 feet. When the sale closed, Mrs. T received over one million dollars in cash, after taxes. I've never seen a client so happy. Twenty-five years later, I still hear from her children.

Practical Tips

When negotiating a Major League Baseball contract for a gifted pitcher, the agent chooses not to stress the benefits to be derived from this player but instead points out simply that the loss of this player's skill will be "outcome-detrimental" to the interested team.[18]

Patience and persistence pay off. Calvin Coolidge said, "Nothing in the world can take the place of persistence. Talent will not. Nothing is more common than unsuccessful men of talent. Genius will not. . . . The world is full of educated derelicts. Persistence and determination alone are omnipotent. The slogan 'Press on' has solved and will always solve the problems of the human race."[19]

ANALYZE FOR ACCURACY

Ever notice how catch phrases are often used to denote a certain authority of a statement, yet, on closer examination, the statement is utterly false? Analyze these catch phrases for accuracy:

- *More criteria* are not always better, regardless of the amount of variables present. The human mind will automatically simplify (sometimes in a manner not intended) what goes into a decision.
- *Reactions to negative and positive consequences* are not always equal. People will risk more to avoid loss than to achieve gain. This loss aversion concept explains why people tend to disfavor a loss more than they favor an equivalent gain.[20] Because

losses loom larger than gains, people are more willing to gamble to avoid them.

One study showed the same people, when asked to avoid a 1-in-1,000 chance of immediate death, wouldn't pay much for an extra fixed margin of safety but demanded huge sums to accept an equal fixed amount of added risk.[21]

"Two things are important to the plaintiff in negotiations: get yourself in the position you want; create fear so opposing counsel is afraid not to settle . . . he may have to pay more later."[22]

- *Lessons of the past* are not always reliable. People cling to them as if everything is repetitive, simple, and without change.
- *Chance* is not always self-correcting. People feel (not think) the previous nine rolls of seven somehow influence the tenth.
- *Splitting the difference is not always fair.* This is a procedural, not a substantive solution, depending on last offers.
- *Back to the Future* vision is not always accurate. People have a tendency to exaggerate in hindsight what could be anticipated in foresight.
- *Playing it safe* is not always the least risky. Taking calculated risks is often the safest thing one can do.
- *Making a decision* does not always clear up a person's thinking. Once the decision is made, rationalization begins to satisfy the person's need to be right, and the mind closes to other alternatives. "The human understanding, when it has once adopted an opinion, draws all thing else to support and agree with it . . . "[23]
- *A logical rational approach* does not always "explain" a feeling. A spreadsheet approach is sometimes too rational; it is only "two-dimensional" and does not show how a person may feel about, and believe in, the decision.
- *Continuing to pressure oneself* to make a decision is not always more effective. Sometimes reducing the pressure allows the best decision to spring up from inside.[24]
- *Highly intuitive people* are not always more reasonable. Intuition gets in the way of reason, talking on two different levels at the same time.[25]

- *Overconfidence* does not always aid in effective evaluation of information. Psychological barriers operate in a similar manner to optical illusions in that they typically involve automatic, subconscious processes that are difficult to subvert. Overconfidence stems, in part, from pervasive biases in the way people pursue and evaluate evidence.[26]
- *Focusing on a particular dispute* does not always mean one will be able to exercise an objective view. In general, people have great difficulty divorcing themselves from their own perspective sufficiently to take an objective view of disputes in which they are involved.[27]
- *With multiple defendants*, it is not always easier to form a consensus on the evaluation of plaintiff's case than to resolve apportionment. Defendants often are more concerned about other defendants "getting off too cheaply."[28]

CONTROL THE PACE

Until we are committed, we have the chance to hesitate or draw back.[29] In criminal defense, the cards are often stacked against us, and we need to level the playing field in order to negotiate from strength. Criminal defense attorneys state that "you must first prepare, prepare, prepare; don't divulge your defenses; remember that practicing criminal law is like practicing law by ambush."[30]

Maintaining Leverage

One approach to controlling the pace of a negotiation is to concentrate on persuading opponents that we maintain the leverage to provide rewards or inflict costs upon them, that opponents have a different level of leverage from what they think they have, and that our settlement range is different from what they think.[31]

This is the art of letting someone else have your way.[32] A good guideline is for the negotiator to advance arguments as though presenting them to an impartial arbitrator. On the receiving side, a good guideline is to listen to arguments as though the negotiator were an impartial arbitrator, remaining open to persuasion despite self-interest and preconceptions.[33]

To maintain leverage, set the pace in advance and determine the opponent's deadline. Change the pace to open opportunities. Reschedule a meeting to alter momentum. Eat a big breakfast to give endurance. But in any case, choose a specific time and location for each negotiation session.

> ***Insights from a Fresh Perspective:*** *Years ago I was taking flying lessons. When I first started flying, I gripped the controls so tightly that my instructor reprimanded me. I loosened up on the controls, but I didn't quite get the point until some weeks later when I went flying with a very experienced pilot. Everything he did was so smooth and controlled. His adjustments on the controls were slight and smooth. He held the yoke loosely, calmly, and confidently. On my next lesson, I imitated his technique with my instructor at my side. Just the act of imitating this great pilot made me a better pilot, and I was instantly more relaxed. My instructor noticed, and he said, "I don't know who you've been flying with, but it's doing you a lot of good." Negotiating can be like this too. You shouldn't grip the problem so tightly that you lose control, and you should imitate the masters to improve your technique.*

Increasing Persuasiveness

Opportunities to increase our persuasiveness sometimes come unexpectedly. They are not labeled. There is no explicit set of instructions on when to expect the unexpected. They come buried in everyday events, in chance occurrences too insignificant to wave a flag over, but these chance occurrences open opportunities. My former senior law partner and a great defense attorney, the late R. J. Vandaworker, was always prepared to negotiate at LSU basketball games if and when the opportunity presented itself. He carefully researched the latest cases just before game time and then created the opportunity during a break by watching and walking toward the concession stand or rest rooms to meet, just by chance, that plaintiff's attorney and say "Have you seen that recent case?"

The wisdom of one diminutive Jedi Master, Yoda, is pertinent: "But beware of the dark side. Anger, fear, aggression; the dark side of the Force are they. Easily they flow, quick to join you in a fight. If once you start down the dark path, forever will it dominate your destiny, consume you it will . . . fear is the path to the dark side. Fear leads to anger. Anger leads to hate. Hate leads to suffering. Do or do not; there is no try."[35]

> ***Insights from a Fresh Perspective:*** *I have learned about components of effective negotiation that are highly crucial to human beings' success both as negotiators and individuals. This reminds me of the experiences I had as a young musician. Being very ambitious, I was educated in Germany by some of the best musicians and finest individuals I have ever met. They taught me how to play the saxophone and the clarinet, gave me the guidance in developing a unique sound, made me familiar with complicated rhythm patterns, and introduced me to some of the greatest pieces of music. Yet, I missed out on the most important lesson they tried to teach me. Since I considered sound, techniques, and rhythms to be separate from each other, I was probably one of the best technically educated musicians of my age. However, I didn't realize that such skills are not ends in themselves but merely means that serve the ultimate goal of making great music. Thus, when combined with emotions, technical skills prove helpful in creating beautiful and unique music. When applying for a well-known orchestra, I was undoubtedly the best applicant in terms of technical skills; nonetheless, I did not get the job. To my surprise, one of my peers, whom I had considered to be 'inferior' to me, was admitted to the orchestra.*
>
> *Against that background, I started to question my courses of action and realized that I had been off the target for years. Even though my technical skills had been better than those of my peers, some of them were still way better musicians than I was since they emotionally linked their skills in order to create music. In retrospect, being rejected proved more helpful; two years later, I got a job with an even better orchestra.*
>
> *This negotiation class and these materials gave me yet another opportunity to question my courses of action, which—to me—was its most striking feature. Rather than providing me with a number of tricks for negotiations, they enabled me to become aware of who*

> *I am, who I want to be, how others perceive me, and what others expect of me. The insight I gained is priceless.*

DEAL WITH DEADLOCK

Dealing with deadlock demands our using the subtleties embedded in the art of persuasion. These include being patient, broadening perspective, preserving relationships, and saying thanks.

Being Patient

Don't rush the closing when there appears to be a deadlock. Be patient. Instead of answering the question, change the topic or switch from a competitive mode to a more cooperative mode (a "softening" or "defusing" technique). President John F. Kennedy stated, "Civility is not a sign of weakness and sincerity is not a matter to be proven. Never negotiate out of fear or fear to negotiate."[36]

> ***Insights from a Fresh Perspective:*** *The word "patience" in Chinese uses as the top character a knife; the bottom character a heart. This Chinese character came from a true story. Thousands of years ago, in ancient China, there were several small nations fighting against each other for control. Zhao, one of the smallest nations is defeated by Qin, the strongest nation at the time. Zhao's King was killed during the war, and Zhao's prince was captured and made a slave to Qin. Qin tried everything he could to torture and humiliate Zhao in order to make him angry and fight back, so Qin would have an excuse to kill him for good. To Qin's surprise, Zhao never argued back, never fought back, no matter how bad he was being treated; he obeyed Qin's orders and served him as if Qin was his King. Every day during the humiliating 10 years, Zhao plans how to get back to his people alive and lead them to fight back for their country. He rehearses thousands of times how he would kill Qin with his own hands. He keeps a knife on top of his heart every night to remind himself to be patient for the right time to defeat such a powerful enemy, because it is so hard and painful not to act on his burning desire to kill his enemy. After being released, he unites with his people, gathers his soldiers and fights back. He defeats Qin and wins*

> *back his country and his crown. Being patient is indeed one of the hardest virtues to master, and it is also one of the most rewarding things. Anxiety and emotion make us blind and deaf. I cannot tell you how many times I act out of my own anxiety and miss out on God's good plans for me.*

Going to the Balcony for Perspective

When facing a difficult negotiation, step back and see the situation objectively. Imagine negotiating on a stage, and then imagine climbing onto a balcony overlooking the stage. The balcony is a metaphor for a mental attitude of detachment. A similar approach is to take a mental helicopter to the ceiling and look down with a sense of humor. In the ancient Japanese art of swordsmanship, students are instructed to look at an opponent as if the opponent were a far-off mountain, a "distanced view of close things." Such is the view from the balcony.[37]

Help the opponent back away without backing down. Deal with deadlock by broadening the domain of negotiations, even where there may be no zone of agreement. Try enlarging the domain of negotiations to include more complicated exchanges (for example, contingency arrangements). Instead of pushing (telling them), mediate the negotiation by living in the open-ended question. Consider combining a number of issues into a single composite text for discussion. It may be easier to talk about a single negotiating proposal rather than two proposals simultaneously.[38]

Practical Tips

Repeat, rephrase, repackage, and reinterpret the question. Back off, smile, wait, be silent, be patient. Explore the reasons for the disagreement, then decide when to argue law, facts, or price.

Give alternatives. Use warnings, not threats. Recognize that sometimes an opponent is more apt to misunderstand and to say "no" on the telephone.

Try restating an opponent's case in the same way the opponent would tell it. Then add one more argument in the opponent's favor. Then wait.

When in doubt about what should be done, do nothing.

Preserving Relationships

Throughout the negotiation of a business transaction, including the post-deal negotiations, the relationship between the parties remains the key element. Relationships can have a profound effect. After the contract has been put in the drawer, what matters most is the relationship. When attention turns from how to share expected profits (when the deal is first negotiated) to how to allocate an expected loss (when the deal turns sour), the importance of this continuing relationship surfaces. Sometimes the aggrieved party assumes part of the loss and views the relationship with the offending party as more valuable than the individual claim arising out of the technical failure to honor the contractual provision.[39]

Relationships continue to have a profound effect on our persuasiveness as negotiators. Just think how often we have savored the special support received from relationships with close friends and relatives, our broader network, and sometimes from an entire community. Malcolm Gladwell, in the introduction to *Outliers: The Story of Success*, describes how a group of immigrants achieved remarkable success in health and business when they formed a close relationship community in Roseta, Pennsylvania. Those people planted vegetable gardens in the long backyards behind their houses, organized festivals, made wine, and built parks and schools. They formed twenty-two civic organizations in a town of just under two thousand people. Researchers in the medical community were dumbfounded when trying to explain why, in this particular group of people living in this small town, no one under the age of fifty-five had died of a heart attack or showed any signs of heart disease. Gladwell explained that these doctors realized that to convince the medical establishment how to understand the situation better,

> They had to get them to realize that they wouldn't be able to understand why someone was healthy if all they did was think about an individual's personal choices or actions in isolation. They had to look beyond the individual. They had to understand the culture he or she was a part of, and who their friends and families were, and what town their families were from. They had to appreciate the idea that the values of the world we inhabit and the people we surround ourselves with have a profound effect on who we are.[40]

Michelangelo has been quoted as having said that inside every block of stone dwells a beautiful statue. All one had to do is remove the excess material to reveal it. Rosamund and Benjamin Zander use this example in *The Art of Possibility* to illustrate the need to recognize the possibilities in others. You do this by "giving them an A." The authors point out that in their approach to others, "You support others to be all they dream of being. The practice of giving an A transports your relationship from the world of measurement into the universe of possibility."[41]

Contrast for a moment those we know who exist in a culture of isolated individualism with those who live surrounded by relationships. People who focus on relationships in work, creativity, and caring and who are embedded in a community of relationships "are both freed and empowered to become who they were born to be." These ideas are developed powerfully by Parker J. Palmer in *The Active Life: A spirituality of Work, Creativity, and Caring.* [42]

> ***Insights from a Fresh Perspective:*** *I see negotiations as a slow dance—even when I am in the midst of a negotiation. I try to accurately envision, (1) what my next move is going to be, (2) my opponent's next move, and then (3) my next move (three steps ahead). This is the exciting part of becoming your own coach. Although I have certainly not mastered the skill, I am beginning to see it from the "mental helicopter" position, and that is exciting—almost like a running back in football who sees the running lane open up in slow motion.*

Saying Thanks

Gratitude works because a feeling of well-being enhances relationships. Sometimes it may even break a deadlock in an ugly negotiation. Gratitude adds meaning to our relationships because it is a key component to a feeling of being respected, to a feeling of being listened to, and to a feeling of being understood. So say thanks whenever it is appropriate.

NOTICE SUBTLE CHANGES IN THE FLOW

To persuade effectively, we must be alert to changes in the flow of information, changes in position, changes in perceptions, and changes in tone, volume, pitch, and tempo. These changes signal the development of a pattern. Listen deeply to detect nuances of non-verbal offers, and recognize patterns indicating that a slight shift in emphasis could lead to a more productive avenue of dialogue. A reluctance to discuss one aspect of the problem is, in a sense, a hidden offer to discuss another.[43]

Generating Language

Wisdom is developed in the brain through conversation, thought, imagination, empathy, and reflection. Preparation results from creating a database containing a wide range of information. In order to benefit the most from changes in the flow of information, we must generate language and actively creative ideas and not just listen and observe passively.[44]

Adapting to Multiparty Negotiations

In multiparty negotiations, the focus needs to be a little different from that used in two-party negotiations. Unique skills and analytical tools are required to deal with coalition formation, problems of process management, and the constantly shifting nature of each party's best alternative to a negotiated agreement. Winning coalitions seek to maximize strength and the chances of a win for coalition members. Blocking coalitions try to protect coalition members' interests that may be threatened by emerging deals. Sometimes it is a distinct advantage to be part of both a winning coalition and a blocking coalition simultaneously.[45]

Practical Tips

An innovative technique used in multi-party negotiations to achieve an internal risk-sharing agreement is for a neutral party to take a pocket calculator, enter a random number not revealed to anyone, and then have each defendant add, secretly, their agreed contribution.

The random number is later deducted in order to determine if the total pot is sufficient to meet the plaintiff's demands. This process is repeated until the pot is right. Then all parties sign an agreement confirming their respective contributions.

Anticipating Professionalism Issues

A key characteristic of the art of persuasion is attitude. Indeed, attitude determines what we stand for as individuals. We must balance our duties—duties to be competent, loyal, and to maintain confidentiality of information; duties as a responsible citizen to uphold the moral values of both community and country; and duties to our religion, family, friends, associates, and ourselves. Personal interests and professional duties interact to create tension, which demands exercising good judgment.

As we take time to think about these things with renewed confidence, we formulate an approach before being confronted with that tough decision. And we shouldn't limit our thinking to just what is required but to what is expected of us as professionals, as Judge Rubin suggested. This involves thinking about affirming timeless values, the subject of our next and final component.

What patterns have you recognized in developing relationships?

Summary

- When persuading, focus on showing, not just telling.
- Give an opponent additional time to answer. Wait, be silent, be patient.
- Be a good record keeper, especially in the presence of an opponent.
- Remember that reaction to negative and positive consequences are not equal. The negative is stronger.
- Maintain control confidently.
- Rely on relationships.
- Be alert to subtle changes in the flow of information.
- Anticipate professionalism issues
- Say thanks. Gratitude works.

NOTES

1. Daniel H. Pink, *A Whole New Mind, Why Right-Brainers Will Rule the Future* (NY: The Penguin Group, 2006), 26.

2. Ibid, 51.
3. Adopted from article by Professor James W. McElhaney, Case Western Reserve University School of Law (Cleveland) and lecturer at South Texas College of Law (Houston), in *ABA Journal*, December 2006.
4. John Powell, *He Touched Me* (Allen, TX: Argus Communication, 1974), 94.
5. Gregory M. Eaton, attorney, Baton Rouge, speaking to the class.
6. Samuel Johnson, *The Free Dictionary*, http://www.thefreedictionary.com/negotiate
7. Aristotle, *Rhetoric* (the Revised Oxford Translation, 1984), 2155.
8. Onora O'Neill, Lecture 1, *The BBC Lecture Series 2002* (Cambridge: Cambridge University Press, 2002).
9. Malcolm Gladwell, *The Tipping Point: How Little Things Can Make a Big Difference* (Boston, Little Brown and Company, 2000), 259.
10. My former senior law partner, R.J. Vandaworker, attorney, Baton Rouge, speaking to the class
11. Gerry Spence, *How to Argue & Win Every Time: At Home, At Work, In Court, Everywhere, Everyday* (New York: St. Martin's Griffin, 1996), 199.
12. "Ready to Start Your Business," *USA Today* (July 2006).
13. Frank Heathrow, attorney, Baton Rouge, speaking to the class.
14. This section adopted from Daniel Yankelovich, *The Magic of Dialogue: Transforming Conflict into Cooperation* (Touchstone, 2001), 12, 14–15.
15. John W. deGravelles, attorney, Baton Rouge, speaking to the class.
16. Virginia Postel, Forbes (August 1998).
17. Adopted from Arno Penzias, astrophysicist, research scientist, Nobel Prize winner for discovery of the background radiation from the 'Big Bang', *Fortune* (January 1996).
18. Tyler Kepner, "In Bidding for Ace," *New York Times*, (November 5, 2006), Section 8, page 1.

19. President Calvin Coolidge, *Silent Cal's Almanac: the Homespun Wit and Wisdom of Vermont's Calvin Coolidge* (David Pietrusza, 2008), 85.
20. John S. Murray, Alan Scott Rau, and Edward F. Sherman, *Negotiation* (Foundation Press, 1996), 9–10, 49.
21. Richard Thaler, *Fortune* (December 9, 2002).
22. Robert E. Pryor, Pryor, Flynn, Priest & Harbor, Attorneys, Knoxville, Speaking to the class.
23. Adopted from graduate comment, LSU 1995.
24. Adopted from graduate comment, LSU 1998.
25. Adopted from Richard Burke and Craig R. Fox, "Psychological Principles in Negotiating Civil Settlements." *Harvard Negotiation Law Review*, Spring 1999.
26. Ibid.
27. Ibid.
28. Robert A. Creo, President of The International Academy of Mediators, Toronto, Canada, speaking at MAPS CLE in New Orleans.
29. Adopted from a presentation by J.W. Goethe, "The Power of Commitment." www.goethesociety.org/pages/quotes.html.
30. Anthony J. Marabella, attorney, Baton Rouge, speaking to the class.
31. ABA Negotiations Seminar, 1985.
32. Daniele Vare, Italian diplomat, quoted by William Ury of Harvard, at negotiation seminar.
33. Professor Roger Fisher of Harvard, speaking at negotiation seminar.
34. Adopted from Adele Scheele, *Skills for Success: A Guide to the Top*, (Morrow, 1979).
35. Jedi Master Yoda's advice to Luke Skywalker in *Star Wars, Episode IV: The Empire Strike Back.*
36. John F. Kennedy, Inaugural Address, January 20, 1961, University Honors.umd.edu/HONR269J/archives/JFK610120.HTM.
37. William Ury, *Getting Past No, Negotiating With Difficult People*, Rev. Ed. (New York: Bantam Books, 1993), 38.
38. Howard Raiffa, John Richardson and David Metcalfe,

Negotiation Analysis: The Science and Art of Collaborative Decision Making (Cambridge, MA: Harvard University Press, 2002), 321–327. This reference discusses the use of the "Single Negotiation Test Process" in the Camp David negotiations between Egypt and Israel, hosted by President Carter on Sept. 18, 1978.

39. Adopted from Professor Jeswald W. Salacuse of Fletcher School of Law at Tufts University in an article in *Negotiation Journal* (October 2001), 315, 319, 321, 324.
40. Gladwell, Malcom, *Outliers, The Story of Success* (New York: Penguin Group, 2008), 10, 11.
41. Rosamund Stone and Benjamin Zander, *The Art of Possibility* (New York: Penguin Group, 2002) 26
42. Parker J. Palmer, *The Active Life: A Spirituality of Work Creativity and Caring* (San Francisco: Jossey-Bass, 1990) 156–57
43. L. Balachandra et. al., in *Negotiation Journal* (October, 2005), 439.
44. Gail Godwin, *Evensong* (Ballantine Books, 2000), 48.
45. L. Susskind, et. al. in *Negotiation Journal* (July, 2005), 396.

Component Ten:

Affirm Timeless Values

Rising to a Higher Level of Consciousness

Our last component of effective negotiating supports all prior components, which, in the beginning, had to be isolated for analysis and study. Now the pieces of the puzzle must be put back together. And we add the critical ingredient found in professionalism: timeless values. These values include courage, loyalty, civility, tolerance, truthfulness, compassion, persistence, and integrity. The timeless-value dimension in negotiations determines relationships, creates power, and forms the very basis for the most important quality: trust. The late Judge Alvin B. Rubin, whose ethical challenge inspired this book, wrote:

> What constitutes a profession is difficult to define comprehensively, but all attempts include reference to a store of special training, knowledge, skills, and to the adoption of ethical standards governing the manner in which these should be employed . . . professionals can be expected to observe something more than the morality of the marketplace. There must be a point at which the lawyer [and I add, any professional] cannot ethically accept an arrangement that is completely unfair to the other side, be that opponent a patsy or a tax collector. . . . This duty of fairness is one owed to the profession and to society: it must supersede any duty owed to the client.[1]

LISTEN TO THE CALL

The word, "vocation" (from *vocare*: "to call") carries a special message. Does this call involve our choosing a vocation, or does it involve a vocation choosing us?

> ***Insights from a Fresh Perspective:*** *The timeless value, "listen to the call," can also be described as choosing a vocation. Steve Jobs spoke on this topic in a commencement address at Stanford University. Jobs relates the story of his ousting from Apple Computer, the company he founded and built into a two-billion dollar corporation in just ten years' time. Although Jobs suffered a public failure, he founded both NEXT Software and Pixar Animation Studios, both becoming successful companies in their own right. In an odd twist of fate, a 1996 merger again made him the CEO of Apple. Jobs had this to say about his professional experience—"I'm convinced that the only thing that kept me going was that I loved what I did. . . . The only way to do great work is to love what you do."*

A senior United States District Court Judge, in a course taught at Duke University, tells about the importance of self-respect:

> You can count on there being a moment in your professional life in which someone is going to ask you to do something wrong. It's going to be an associate, a client, or someone else. . . . At that moment, your future hangs in the balance. You either say yes or no. You may have three kids at home and a mortgage that you've got to worry about, but there's only one answer, 'No.' . . . If you say, 'Yes, I'll do it,' you might not get caught . . . but you have lost one of the most precious ingredients . . . and that is self-respect.[2]

Choosing Which Voices to Listen to

How often do we recall voices from the past? These are voices of teachers, coaches, and parents who made us truly stop and think. We hear the voice of friends and relatives, the voice from a familiar writing, the voice of authority, and the many voices of experience. What voice do we listen to?[3] This question underscores the recurring theme of this book: we must train and educate our informed intuition as to the timeless values we wish to affirm. This enables us to use them with confidence in a crisis.

Fredrick Buechner points out that a person's life is full of internal and external voices that call from every direction. The more alive and alert people are, the more clamorous their life is. When people are young, their hearing, in some ways, is at its best. Yet we risk our ears by listening to the great, blaring voice of mass culture. This voice threatens to deafen us all with the relentless blasting of the message that we work only to increase salary and status. For everybody, there comes a point of no return, a point beyond which they no longer have life enough left to go back and start all over again.[4] An Eastern philosopher states, "the effects of our actions may be postponed but they are never lost. There is an inevitable reward for good deeds and inescapable punishment for bad. Meditate upon this truth, and seek always to earn good wages from Destiny."[5]

Tragic and true is the conclusion that why so many people fail in life is because they are not aware when they have reached the point in which they are still free to act according to reason and core values. They are aware of this choice only after it is too late to make a decision.[6]

Warren Buffett, a successful business executive, describes it another way. Buffett points out that the chains of habit are too light to be felt until they are too heavy to be broken. We get older and can't change many of our habits. But younger people will have the habits twenty years from now that they decide to put into practice today.[7]

> ***Insights from a Fresh Perspective:*** *The convictions that we build for ourselves act as a lighthouse when we can't see the shoreline. Personal doubt can be the shadow obscuring our vision, keeping us from knowing the right direction. The values that we adopt will be a beacon leading us down our life's path—the correct path.*

Using Ethical Instinct

Using ethical instinct is illustrated by the great, mythical golf match in the movie *The Legend of Bagger Vance* (2002). The match involves golf greats Walter Hagan, Bobby Jones, and a local golfer who, ahead by one stroke, calls a one-stroke penalty on himself for the slight movement of his ball just before he hits it. The match ends in a tie. Our local golfer does not win the match, but when he is perched on the brink of the rest of his life, he is clear with his conscience and happy that he let ethical instincts prevail.

In life, we constantly prepare for moments and events. We worry about things, think about injustices, and search for answers in Tolstoy and Ruskin. Then, all of a sudden, the issue is not whether we agree with what we have heard and read and studied. The issue is ourselves and what we have become.[8]

> ***Insights from a Fresh Perspective:*** *There are two types of training in karate: Karate-jitsu and Karate-do. Karate-jitsu is simply the physical act of learning Karate with no emphasis on character or morality. This type of training is likely to lead to the misuse of karate techniques as the practitioner has no compass to find the right way.*
>
> *Karate-do, which translates "the way of the empty hand," requires the training of one's mind, spirit, and body. In many ways, the physical attributes of Karate-do (for example, blocking, punching, kicking) are merely a byproduct of training the mind and spirit. In this type of training, the students are learning respect, self-control, integrity, and humility. Karate-do better prepares students to make correct moral decisions when practicing Karate.*
>
> *Negotiating seems to be the same. If you simply learn tactics, you could stray down the path of questionable moral decisions, which ultimately would lead to your own downfall. However, if you ground your negotiating tactics within the boundaries of morality, fairness and justice, you will be better equipped to recognize immoral decisions and have the wisdom to resist them.*

Making Responsible Choices

If we hope to make responsible choices, we must first seek an inner freedom so as not to be overly influenced by subconscious motivations that could direct decisions without our awareness. We must screen with our heart what we discover with our mind and, most importantly, use a sound value system.[9]

When life asks us to make choices, how do we weigh our options with respect to what is important? What value do we place on creativity, making more money, social status, helping others, the satisfaction of contributing to a larger system of which we are a part? To rely on our value system, we must have faith in that system and faith in ourselves, in our ability to act on that value system.

Parker J. Palmer states, "Every form of power contains its own moral trajectory, an ethical course and objective from which it is not likely to be deflected."[10]

Not Giving Little Answers to Big Questions

When we become professionals, we should be sensitive to the tendency some people have to give little answers to the profound questions which confront them. We need to reflect on our methods of decision-making. Determine whether we are using all of the ingredients—our minds and intellects, our hearts and emotions, our experiences and training, and, most importantly, a timeless value system that puts the odds in our favor.

Years ago there were two men in the posh club car on a train whizzing through the Midwest.[11] One of the men begins to muse to himself, "This is a fantastic train, an amazing way to travel, but some day it is going to be rust, in the trash heap . . . all these people in here, sipping their scotch and having a friendly card game are going to be dust." Looking out at the farmlands flashing by in a blur, he glances up to his buddy and says, "Hey Joe, . . . where . . . are we going?" Joe slowly looks up from his newspaper and says, "You know, Mike, we're going to Omaha." How often do we tend to give an Omaha kind of answer to the big questions?

In the movie *To Kill a Mockingbird* (1962), which was based on Harper Lee's Pulitzer Prize winning novel, Tom Robinson is wrongfully found guilty of assault despite the valiant efforts of defense attorney Atticus Finch (played by Gregory Peck) in the jam-packed courtroom. By asking carefully constructed questions, Atticus has, in fact, shown that his client did not, and because of a lame arm, could not, have delivered the blow. Nonetheless, the jury finds him guilty as charged. Judge Taylor has completed polling the jury, and the milling crowd has now departed. Atticus' children remain seated in the balcony, watching the proceedings below. As they see their father walk slowly out of the courtroom, an elderly gentleman nudges them, saying, "Miss Jean Louise, stand up. Your father is passing." What a wonderful display of respect prompted by the father's deep commitment to timeless values. He loses the case but wins in the eyes of those around him.

> ***Insights from a Fresh Perspective:*** *Raised in India, I grew up with cousins, aunts, uncles, and many others. I was taught the values of peaceful co-existence, quality of sharing, and respect for elders. In India, we respect even objects, like books, as the source of knowledge. Likewise, a dancer bows to the stage, a farmer to his yoke, and a truck driver to his truck, and so on. The significance of "OM," or the absolute, has made me understand that all of us belong to the same system. These values helped me adapt to a totally different culture. Just as important, learning the Indian values allowed me to see differences in people while remembering that we are all the same.*

Seeing with One-Minute Wisdom

By adopting a sound value system before we negotiate, we gain insight to anticipate and recognize compromising situations. We hear our intellect and heart sounding the alarm that tunes us into our value system and gives way to the moral inner voice. We seek to be not just a good negotiator who is trying to be a moral person, but a moral person who is trying to be a good negotiator.

"Is there such a thing as one minute wisdom?" asked a student. "There certainly is," said the Master. The student responded, "But surely one minute is too brief?" The Master replied, "It is fifty-nine seconds too long." The Master then said, "How much time does it take to catch sight of the moon? . . . Opening your eyes may take a lifetime. Seeing is done in a flash."[12]

COMMUNICATE VALUES WITH CONVICTION AND COURAGE

The root of the word "professionalism" means to profess, to affirm, to validate, to confirm. The primary role of a professional, therefore, is to care and to find a way to communicate caring.[13]

A brass plaque at the entrance of the LSU Law School contains these words: "Is it not the duty of the men and women of the law to be concerned with the relationship of morality and ethics to the law?"[14] Practicing attorneys continue with this thought, "You are entering into a profession which is in crisis because too many people are not thinking about ethics."[15]

The only thing truly worth envying is peace of mind that comes as a result of having values and adhering to them.[16] Remember, we don't have to be disagreeable to disagree,[17] and negotiation success many times is attributed to the competence and values of our adversaries.[18]

Letting Reputation Lead

Research shows that different parts of the world fit together from the microscopic universe locked within to the unbounded world of the Internet. Each is part of a large cluster, the worldwide social net from which no one is left out. There is a path between any two people, estimated at a mere six degrees of separation.[19]

It follows, therefore, that as we become part of a group negotiating regularly in a community, our reputation precedes us with amazing speed. "You never forget someone who has treated you unfairly."[20] One of my law partners states, "You always lead with your reputation. . . . People know I am a straight shooter. I feel secure that people know this. You need to determine in your own mind what is right, and, if necessary, settle this point with the client. It is your call, not your client's call."[21]

A highly respected older attorney says, "If you don't trust your opponents, don't reveal facts because it is not likely you will receive theirs. But don't ever put yourself in a position of not telling the truth. If you have confidence in your opponents, then negotiate, first put things on the table and swap information, always telling the truth."[22]

A young attorney states, "You negotiate over problems; but with people, it is important to know who you are as a person and who your opponent is as a person."[23]

> ***Insights from a Fresh Perspective:*** *Each of us has a set of values—what is important to us. Through interpreting different cultures, I*

> *have discovered that our core values are the same. We did not have to "find" timeless values to be able to negotiate—timeless values "found" us a long time ago.*

There is a close relationship between moral reasoning, moral conviction, and moral courage. C. S. Lewis states that, "Courage is not simply one of the virtues but the form of every virtue at the testing point."[24] A missionary and philosopher states that "the more society becomes technical, the more need there is for a counselor with courage."[25] My former rector states that "the best learning is not just a matter of collecting facts, but of forming character."[26]

In my years of law practice, I found that clients wanted me to communicate values with conviction and courage, even if they didn't always say so. Sometimes they would ask me to do something that they didn't really expect me to do. They would say, "Now look, we want to do this fast, and this is how we are going to get around it, okay?" I would pause and say, "You know we can't do that." After a longer pause, they would look me in the eye and say, "Bill, I thought you would say that."

BECOMING A PERSON OF INTEGRITY

A graduating class at the University of South Carolina was told the following:

> As responsibility is passed to your hands, it will not do, as you live the rest of your life, to assume that someone else will bear the major burdens, that someone else will demonstrate the key convictions, that someone else will run for office, that someone else will take care of the poor, that someone else will visit the sick, protect civil rights, enforce the law, preserve culture, transmit value, maintain civilization, and defend freedom. You must never forget that what you do not value will not be valued, that what you do not remember will not be remembered, that what you do not change will not be changed, and that what you do not do will not be done.[27]

Albert Schweitzer, the famous writer, medical doctor, theologian, and musician declared, "I don't know what your destiny will be, but one thing I do know: The only ones among you who will be really happy are those who will have sought and found how to serve."[28]

A former student who joined his family law firm founded by his grandfather returned to the class years later and gave the following presentation, entitled "How do I play by the Rules?":

> Lawyers must have a framework to function within because we are dealing with ethical issues all the time. The Multi-state Professional Responsibility Examination (MPRE) doesn't test your integrity, but how close you can get, how you can operate on the edge. The first thing you should do is decide in your gut what is right and wrong about your case. Focus first on principles of fair play and your conscience, then look up the law. . . . React early to questions of ethics. When it is in your head, react. Practicing law will not make you a person of integrity but will test your integrity. The people of greatest character are lawyers. They get tested every day. It's neat to know people like that because the practice will purify you or burn you up. Character is built every day and is a result of inwardly living good principles. Therefore, it stands to reason that character will not exist when good principles have failed to take up residence in a person's mind, heart, and gut. I plan to be a man of character some day, and I keep trying and I encourage you to do the same. Know what you believe in and hold on tight. Don't let us be your standard, raise the standard! That's what will save this profession.[29]

Having Conviction

Thomas Jefferson, in the Declaration of Independence, spoke of truths, which are self-evident: "Life, liberty, and the pursuit of happiness." Jefferson did not say, "Life, liberty, and property." Instead, he used "pursuit of happiness." This implies a concept of right and obligation to live as we should because living a moral life supposes an obligation to use our freedom correctly.[30]

> ***Insights from a Fresh Perspective:*** *There is a common belief in Ethiopia that if you make a wish whenever you see a meteorite, your dream will come true. I never believed this, yet, each time I saw a meteorite, I wished for something, something I deeply wanted in my life. Now after many years, most of my dreams have come true. The reality is that most of my dreams came true because I worked hard for them, not because I wished at the right moment. I believe*

> *that having strong convictions is what makes one successful, not just making a wish. But whenever I see a meteorite I still look up.*

LET VALUES CONTROL EMOTIONAL REACTIONS

Why does our reasoning tend to support (and not challenge) goals that spring from emotions? Why do our emotions and feelings override our reason?[31] Is there a tension between our intellectual desires and emotional desires that can effectively be handled through a strong commitment to timeless values?

Strong emotional desires, according to William B. Irvine[32], have been hard-wired in us as a result of the evolutionary process of natural selection preserving traits needed for survival. Because of this, reasoning has a tendency to support (rather than question, contradict, or challenge) the goals set by emotional desires. This, in turn, results in misjudgment because the mind and reason operate behind a distorting and accommodating lens of emotion. People think they are making good, sound decisions based on a well-reasoned process, but the truth often is that people have fooled themselves. Irvine argues that unless emotions commit to the goals our set by our intellect it is unlikely that we will accomplish the goals set by our intellect. In other words, the best intellectual strategy for counteracting a possible veto by emotions is to couple a strong emotional desire to our intellectual desire.

Looking for New Layers of Meaning

A fitting sequel to our earlier story, *The Wizard of Oz*, is the Biblical parable "The Prodigal Son." It tells about a younger son who wants independence, demands his inheritance, and leaves his father and older brother on the farm. The more lost the younger son feels, the more he celebrates. But the voice of the father's heart overtakes the younger son in the far country and tells him, "You can come home, son. Come home!" (The Greek word for "come" also means "go"). The younger son comes to his senses and returns with a forgiveness pitch carefully rehearsed. The loving father who has been watching each day for the younger son's return sees a movement on the road. The father recognizes his son, even though he is still a great way off, and runs to greet him (despite the custom that old men in long robes don't run). The father brushes aside the rehearsed forgiveness pitch and orders a big celebration because his son who was lost has been found. The older son, who has stayed home and been faithful to his father, resents the celebration.

Over a time span of 330, years this parable uniquely touched the lives of three men shortly before they died.

First is Rembrandt Van Rijn (1606–1669), a talented Dutch painter, who sought to reveal something deeper in the facial expressions of his subjects through the use of rich layers of translucent paint. His painting entitled "Return of the Prodigal Son" depicts a blind old man with a bedraggled youngster kneeling and being pressed inward by the old man's hands. When Rembrandt created this painting, he was losing his sight. His wife and seven children were dead. He was bankrupt; his paintings and supplies had been seized. Yet in this, one of his last paintings, he depicts himself as the forgiving father with the younger son kneeling at his feet with an upturned, battered shoe. The imagery is breathtaking with the father's masculine right hand gripping the son's left shoulder, and a feminine left hand gently pressing the son inward toward the womb. So the father is also a mother figure. A Russian guidebook points out that the painting draws the final balance of Rembrandt's life: the artist is left alone, stripped of all earthly pleasures apart from the capacity to create. The emotions that pervade all of Rembrandt's work—love, suffering, and forgiveness—reach their greatest intensity in this painting.

Second is Henri J. M. Nouwen (1932–1996), a Dutch Catholic priest who taught at Notre Dame, Yale, and Harvard, a renowned writer who authored numerous books on spirituality. One of Nouwen's last books, *Return of the Prodigal: A Story of Homecoming,* describes Nouwen's experience in seeing a copy of this painting in a graduate student's study and taking a trip to view the original. Nouwen wrote about the life-changing effect of viewing the 6' x 9' original in the Hermitage, St. Petersburg, Russia, and how it spoke so forcefully to him about the journey of life. He dedicated the book to his own father for his father's 90th birthday.[33]

Third is Dr. Joseph William Reddoch Jr. (1934–1997), an ophthalmologist in New Orleans, one of my best friends, who gave me a copy of Nouwen's book. Reddoch's skill as an eye surgeon and patient counselor was surpassed only by his great insight that this painting's story would speak so strongly to me. The force of Reddoch's story is its subtlety. Reddoch was the picture of health. He was upbeat, active, and very excited about his brother giving him a new kidney. He came to visit me in the country. We walked in the woods and around the fishpond. He told me I must read an unusual book that he would send me about Rembrandt's painting. Reddoch's story takes a sudden turn. His son called early in the morning on the day of the scheduled kidney transplant operation to say that, three hours before the operation, his dad died very unexpectedly. At his funeral in the large St. Charles Presbyterian Church in New Orleans, there were hundreds of people I had never seen before. I later learned that Reddoch was loved by these people, not only because he had restored their sight but because of the way he had listened to them and made them feel.

In 2006, I was a seminar speaker for the University of Tennessee College Law on a Baltic cruise and had the good fortune to go to the Hermitage to see for myself the original painting. I was struck by the depth of feeling, particularly in the eyes and hands of the aging father. Remaining in my spot near the painting as each tour group approached, I listened carefully to what the English-speaking guides said. Several mentioned that Rembrandt was so moved when he finished the painting that he reached over and pressed his thumbprint on the bottom of the heel of the prodigal son's up turned, battered shoe. I looked more carefully and could just barely see a smudge on the heel.

Long after their deaths, each at about age sixty-three, these men continue to contribute a tone, part of a harmony, that helps me see new layers of meaning in this parable: Rembrandt, through the tip of an artist's paintbrush; Nouwen, through the point of a writer's pen; and Reddoch, through the edge of an eye-surgeon's scalpel.

Nouwen explains it best in pointing out that each of us wants to return to be patted on the shoulder and congratulated for our past accomplishments. And, at some point in time, we play the part of the restless young son, the resentful older son, and the compassionate father. But everyone—I, you, all of us—should focus on returning home, not to be patted on the back and congratulated by the father, but to become the father.

RISE TO A HIGHER LEVEL OF CONSCIOUSNESS

When considering the role of timeless values and the need for us to rise to a higher level of consciousness, it is helpful to take time to notice examples of symmetry, harmony, and uniform proportions in the world around us, which helps us add a new dimension to our understanding. Repeating proportions (such as 1.618, the Divine Proportion, also known as the Golden Section or Golden Ratio) in sunflowers, pineapples, rose petals, pine cones, seashells, and in heavenly bodies, point to uniformities in nature.

Recognizing Uniformities in Nature

As pointed out by Priya Hemingway in *Divine Proportion,* early Greeks recognized this constant proportion in nature, musical harmony, and in mathematics; and, intuitively "understood proportion to be a relationship in which differences are part of the whole."[34] The author continued, "And how else but through proportion could creation reflect the creator? What we discover, whether we look toward the macrocosm or toward the microcosm, is an existence in which everything is perfectly proportioned. . . . Looking at small things and contemplating them helps us to see bigger things more clearly."[35]

Just as certain ratios exist in the smallest DNA molecule and the largest spiral galaxy, including our own Milky Way, so do timeless values exist. I have used the spiral symbol of the Divine Proportion to serve as a reminder of our need as negotiators to affirm timeless values. Anderson Scott Olsen, in *The Golden Section: Nature's Greatest Secret,* states in the conclusion, "it is humanity's duty to reconnect and resonate with this deep code of nature, beautifying our world and our relationships with . . . golden standards of excellence."[36]

Adding New Dimensions

Each of our negotiations adds new dimension to our understanding. We continue connecting the dots on our graph of experience. We try to remain open to things that we have excluded, to stay curious, and to look for what we can do to help though we may not yet know how. Our attention is drawn to the cowboy of the West, where a man's word is his bond and a handshake is enough to seal any agreement.[37]

As Kahlil Gibran (1883–1931) observed, "Life is that which we see and experience through the spirit; but the world around us we come to know through our understanding and reason."[38]

> ***Insights from a Fresh Perspective:*** *A culmination of understanding occurred for me in the final component where the question was posed, "Now, do you see a pattern more clearly?" What was once an abstract concept had become conceptual. A pattern in itself is an element of a set. Once the elements are understood, their predictive value allows for the development of a model. The model can then be used as a tool in the negotiation process to get to a dimension where underlying realities are revealed. In this dimension, a great deal of intellectual truth occurs but it is important to apply this knowledge. Constantin Brancusi, a former Romanian sculptor said, "Theories are patterns without value. What counts is action."*

Recurring patterns in our consideration of these ideas linking the negotiator mind-set with timeless values have shown us the shape of the river, the big picture. We see more clearly what Robert Frost meant when he wrote, "My object in living is to unite my avocation and my vocation as my two eyes make one in sight."[39]

President Barack H. Obama, the 2009 Nobel Peace Prize winner, in his 2009 Inaugural Address, confirms our focus on timeless values in professionalism. "Our challenges may be new. The instruments with which we meet them may be new. But those values upon which our success depends—honesty and hard work, courage and fair play, tolerance and curiosity, loyalty and patriotism—these things are old. These things are true."[40]

Now, do you see a pattern more clearly?

Summary

- Anticipate moral dilemmas and rehearse your answer.
- Look for leading lessons to be learned.
- Ask questions and observe in order to isolate and understand moral issues.
- Commit emotionally to timeless values as a way to control undesirable emotional reactions.
- Trust your ethical instinct as you rise to a higher level of consciousness.
- Remember that the forces of tough competitiveness and professionalism exist in a state of tension, and in a state of unity.

NOTES

1. Alvin B. Rubin, Judge, U.S. 5th Circuit Court of Appeals; Professor-Adjunct LSU Law Center, *Teaching Legal Negotiations*, 35 LLR 577 (1975), 578–79.
2. Judge William M. Hoeveler, senior judge of the U.S. District Court in Miami who presided over the Noriega trial, quoted in *ABA Journal*, (August 1998), 48, 54.
3. Adopted from a talk by the Reverend Hill Riddle, former Rector of Trinity Church, New Orleans, speaking at Cashiers Summer Chapel.
4. Adopted from Frederic Buechner, former chaplain at Phillips Exeter Academy, New Hampshire, in *The Hungering Dark* (New York: Harper and Row, 1985), 28, 29–30.
5. Fu Wu Ming, http://www.iwise.com/Fu_Wu_Ming
6. Adopted from Eric Fromm, *The Heart of Man* (San Fransisco: HarperCollins Publishers, 1988), 133–43.
7. Warren Buffett, chairman of Berkshire Hathaway Inc., adapted from an interview in *Fortune*, July 20, 1998, 52.
8. Adopted from Steven Pressfield, *The Legend of Bagger Vance; Golf and the Game of Life* (New York: William Morrow and Company, 1995), 203–6.
9. Pierre Wolf, *Discernment: The Art of Choosing Well* (New

York: Penguin, 2000), 6, 15.

10. Parker J. Palmer, *The Active Life: A Spirituality of Work, Creativity, and Caring* (Jossey-Bass, 1999), 109.
11. Idea inspired by James W. Jeans, Sr., in his talk entitled "Advice to Aspiring Advocates" and taped by The Professional Education Group.
12. Adopted from Anthony de Mello, *One Minute Wisdom* (Image, 1988), 1, 97.
13. Adopted from Merrilyn Astin Tarlton, *Law Practice Management*, July/August 1997.
14. Paul M. Hebert, brass plaque at entrance to the Paul M. Herbert Law Center at LSU.
15. Michael C. Palmintier, attorney, Baton Rouge, speaking to the class.
16. Harry Stein, *Ethics [and other Liabilities]: Trying to Live Right in an Amoral World* (New York: 1983), 75.
17. Roger Fisher and William Ury, interview in *The Academy of Management Executive* (August, 2004).
18. Harry Ogden, Baker, Donelson, Bearman, Caldwell & Berkowitz, PC, attorneys, Knoxville, speaking to the class.
19. Albert-Laszlo Barabasi, *Linked: How Everything is Connected to Everything Else and What it for Business, Science, and Everyday Life* (New York: Penguin, 2003). Barabasi is a professor of physics at Notre Dame University.
20. Charles F. Thensted, attorney, New Orleans, speaking to the class.
21. Harry J. "Skip" Philips, attorney, Baton Rouge, one of my law partners, speaking to the class.
22. Ashton L. Stewart, attorney, Baton Rouge, speaking to the class.
23. Robert S. Dampf, Attorney, Lake Charles, speaking to the class.
24. C. S. Lewis, http://www.quotationspage.com/quote37800.html.
25. The Reverend Jak Seynaeve, D.D., formerly with White Fathers of Africa, Professor of Philosophy, LSU, speaking to the class.

26. The Reverend Kenneth Dimmick, former Rector of Grace Church, St. Francisville, Louisiana.
27. Challenge to 1992 graduating class of University of South Carolina by Alexander M. Sanders, Jr., Chief Judge of the South Carolina Court of Appeals.
28. Albert Schweitzer, http://www.quotationsbook.com/quote/18517.html
29. J. Barrett Benton, former LSU student; attorney, Baton Rouge, speaking to the class.
30. Adopted from lecture by Professor J. Rufus Fears, University of Oklahoma, taped and produced by The Teaching Company.
31. William B. Irvine, *On Desire: Why We Want What We Want* (New York: Oxford University Press, 2006), 133.
32. Ibid., 73–76, 106, 116.
33. Henri Nouwen, *Return of the Prodigal: A Story of Homecoming* (New York: Doubleday/Image, 1994), 12, 15, 49.
34. Priya Hemingway, *Divine Proportion* (Sterling Publishing Company Inc., NY, 2005), 181.
35. Ibid., 183.
36. Scott Olsen, *The Golden Section: Nature's Greatest Secret* (Wooden Books Ltd., 2006), 50. See also, H.E. Huntley, *The Divine Proportion: A Study in Mathematical Beauty* (Dover Publications, 1970); Mario Livio, *The Golden Ratio; The Story of Phi; World's Most Astounding Number* (Broadway Books, 2002).
37. James P. Owen, *Cowboy Ethics: What Wall Street can Learn from the Code of the West* (Ketchum, ID: Stoecklein Publishing, 2005), 1, 2. Of particular interest is the author's comment, "I have come to realize that anybody can make money; it is much harder to make a difference."
38. Kahlil Gibran, *The Voice of the Master* (New York Citadel, Carol Publishing Group, 1992), 16.
39. Robert Frost, *Collected Poems, Prose and Plays* (Literary Classics of the United States, 1995), 251–252. The last words of this poem following the quote are, "Only where love and need are one,/And the work is play for mortal stakes,/Is the deed

ever really done/For Heaven and the future's sakes."

40. President Barack H. Obama's Inaugural Address entitled "All This We Will Do," given January 20, 2009, published in *The New York Times,* Wednesday January 21, 2009.

Conclusion:

Ending with Your Final Word

You have the final word because only you can improve your skills as a negotiator. Although a significant part of these skills is mechanical, the rest is informed intuition—an insight, a mind-set, a "feel of things," which you control. Your success as a negotiator does not rest solely on how well you use these skills but on how much your opponent trusts you as an individual. This trust rests on your reputation for adhering to timeless values found in professionalism.

As a skilled negotiator, you distinguish between seeking more facts to have increased information and seeking more insights to have an increased understanding. Becoming more enlightened is achieved when, in addition to knowing the facts presented, you make the connection; you discover how all of it fits. And you apply practical principles and become more effective in using your feelings and emotions. You use your reasoning, your imagination, and your emotions to gain this understanding. You become not just more knowledgeable but wiser in the sense that you are more deeply aware of the connections, of the patterns, and of the great enduring timeless values affecting our lives.

While reading this book, you have contributed greatly to the interpretation of these ideas by using your own unique experience and perspective as a lens to filter these ideas into a valuable asset that can only enhance your future effectiveness as a negotiator. You now have your own answers from your own perspective.

In the beginning, the insight gained from the riverboat pilot was to learn the basics, file away facts and concepts for immediate retrieval, recognize predictable patterns in the negotiation process, see connections among different areas of knowledge, and trust the informed intuition that already exists within. You have developed a database so vast and varied that it supplies you with additional leverage as a negotiator.

It is now time to translate these concepts and Judge Rubin's challenge into practice. It is up to you. Put the handshake back in negotiating. Remember that you have the final word and, like the riverboat pilot, you must know the shape of the river . . . the ever-changing patterns . . . because when it's dark and foggy, that's all you can go by.

BIBLIOGRAPHY

Adams, James L. *Conceptual Blockbusting: A Guide to Better Ideas.* Reading, MA: Addison-Wesley Publishing Company, 1995.

Adler, Rosen, and Silverstein. "Emotions in Negotiation." *Negotiation Journal* (April 1998).

Alfini, James J., et. al. *Mediation Theory and Practice. Lexis Publishing,* 2001.

Allison, John R. *Harvard Business Review on Negotiation and Conflict Resolution.* Boston, MA: Harvard Business School Publishing, 2000.

Argyle, Michael. "Cultural Differences in Bodily Communication." *Bodily Communication,* 2nd Ed. London: Methuen & Co. Ltd., 1988.

Barabasi, Albert-Laszlo. *Linked: How Everything is Connected to Everything Else and What It Means for Business, Science and Everyday Life.* New York: Penguin, 2003.

Barone, Michael. *Hard America, Soft American: Competition vs. Coddling and the Battle for the Nations Future.* New York: Three Rivers Press, 2005.

Barratt, Krome. *Logic and Design: The Syntax of Art, Science & Mathematics.* Bernardsville, NJ: Eastview Editions, 1980.

Bastress, Robert M. and Joseph D. Harbaugh. *Interviewing, Counseling and Negotiating Skills for Effective Representation.* Boston, MA: Little Brown & Company, 1990.

Bazerman and Neale. *Negotiating Rationally.* Simon & Schuster, Inc., 1992.

Bellow, Gary. *Lawyering Process: Negotiation.* West Publishing Group, 1981.

Benoliel, Michael. *Done Deal: Insights from Interviews with the World's Best Negotiators.* Cincinnati, OH: Adams Media Corporation, 2004.

Berman, Maureen and I. William Zartman. *The Practical Negotiator.* New Haven, CT: Yale University Press, 1983.

Berthoff, Ann E. *The Making of Meaning: Metaphors, Models and Maxims for Writing Teachers.* Portsmouth, NH: Boynton/Cook

Publishers, 1981.

Blanchard, Ken. *Playing the Great Game of Golf: Making Every Minute Count* (Quill, 1994).

Blanchard, Kenneth and Norman Vincent Peale. *The Power of Ethical Management*. New York: William Morrow and Company, 1988.

Blanchard, Kenneth H. and Spencer Johnson. *One Minute Manager*. 2nd Ed. New York: HarperCollins Business, 2000.

Bok, Sissela. *Lying: Moral Choice in Public and Private Life*. New York, Random House/Vintage, 1999.

Boomer, Percy. *On Learning Golf*. Rev. Ed. Classics of Golf, 2007.

Brooks, David. "Teaching the Elephant." *The New York Times* (December 3, 2006).

Carter, Stephen L. "The Insufficiency of Honesty." *Atlantic Monthly* (February, 1996).

Churchman, David. *Negotiation: Process, Tactics, Theory*. Lanham MD, 1995.

Cohen, Herb. *You Can Negotiate Anything: How To Get What You Want*. Lyle Stuart, 1980.

Collins, Jim. *Good to Great: Why Some Companies Make the Leap . . . and Others Don't*. New York: HarperCollins Publishers, 2001.

Coquillette, Daniel R. *Lawyers and Fundamental Moral Responsibility: Materials*. 2nd Ed. Cincinnati, OH: Anderson Publishing Company; 1995.

Covey, Stephen R. *Seven Habits of Highly Effective People: Powerful Lessons in Personal Change*. Free Press, 1989.

Craver, Charles B. *Effective Legal Negotiation and Settlement*. 2nd Ed. The Michie Co., 1993.

Dauer, Edward A. *Alternative Dispute Resolution Law and Practice*. Juris Publishing, 2000.

de Mello, Anthony. *One Minute Wisdom*. Image, 1988.

de Saint-Exupéry, Antoine. *The Little Prince*. Harvest Books, 2000.

Dickens, Charles. *Hunted Down: The Detective Stories of Charles Dickens*. Dufour, 2006.

Dubos, René. *A God Within*. New York: Scribner, 1984.

Edwards, Betty. *Drawing on the Artist Within*. Fireside, 1987.

______Drawing on the Right Side of the Brain. Rev. Ed. New York: Tarcher/Penguin USA, 1989.

Edwards, Harry and James White. *The Lawyer as a Negotiator.* West Publishing Co., 1977.

Elbow, Peter and Pat Belanoff. *Being a Writer: A Community of Writers Revisited.* McGraw-Hill, 2002.

Eiseley, Loren C. *The Unexpected Universe.* New York: Harcourt, 1972.

Ervin, Sam J. *Humor of a Country Lawyer.* Chapel Hill: University of North Carolina Press, 1994.

Fisher, Robert and William Ury. *Getting to Yes: Negotiating Agreement Without Giving In.* Boston, 1981.

Fisher and Brown. *Getting Together: Building Relationships as we Negotiate.* Penguin, 1938.

Fisher, Kopelman, and Schneider. *Beyond Machiavelli: Tools for Coping With Conflict.* Cambridge, MA, Harvard Press, 1994.

Fisher, Roger and Daniel Shapiro. *Beyond Reason: Using Emotions As You Negotiate.* New York: Viking, 2005.

Florida, Richard. *The Rise of the Creative Class, and How It's Transforming Work, Leisure, Community and Everyday Life.* New York: Basic Books, 2002.

Frankfurt, Harry G. *On Bullshit.* Princeton, NJ: Princeton University Press, 2005.

______On Truth. New York: Alfred A. Knopf, 2006.

Frankl, Viktor E. *Man's Search for Meaning.* Boston: Beacon Press, 2006.

Frascogna and Hetherington. *Negotiation Strategy for Lawyers.* Prentice-Hall, 1984.

Freund, James C. *Lawering: A Realistic Approach To Legal Practice.* Law Journal Seminars-Press, 1979.

Gallwey, W. Timothy. *The Inner Game of Golf.* New York: Random House, 1998.

______*The Inner Game of Tennis,* New York: Random House, 1997.

Gelfand, Michele J. and Jeanne M. Brett, ed. *The Handbook of Negotiation and Culture.* Stanford, CA: Stanford University Press, 2004.

Gifford, Donald G. *Gifford's Legal Negotiation Theory and Applications*. New York: West Publishing, 2001.

Gladwell, Malcolm. *Blink: the Power of Thinking Without Thinking*. Boston: Little, Brown and Company, 2005.

______*The Tipping Point: How Little Things Can Make a Big Difference*. Boston: Little, Brown and Company, 2000.

______*Outliers, The Story of Success*. New York: Penguin Group, 2008.

Godwin, Gail. *Evensong*. Ballentine Books, 2000.

Golann, Dwight and Marjorie Corman Aaron. *Mediating Legal Disputes: Effective Strategies for Lawyers and Mediators*. Aspen Publishers Inc., 1996.

Guerrero, Laura K. and Kory Floyd. "Interpersonal Deception." *Nonverbal Communication in Close Relationships*. Mahwah, NJ: Lawrence Erlbaum Associates, Publishers, 2006.

Hambidge, Jay. *The Elements of Dynamic Symmetry*. Mineola, NY: Dover Publications, 1967.

Haydock, Roger S. *Negotiation Practice*. John Wiley & Sons, 1984.

Hawking, Stephen W. *The Universe in a Nutshell*. Bantam, 2001.

Hemingway, Ernest. *A Moveable Feast*. New York: Scribner, 1992.

Hemingway, Priya. *Divine Proportion*. New York: Sterling Publishing, 2005.

Hendel, Richard. *On Book Design*. New Haven, CT: Yale University Press, 1998.

Hermann, Phillip J. *Better Settlements Through Leverage*. Aqueduct Books, 1965.

Herrigel, Eugen. *Zen in the Art of Archery*. Vintage, 1999.

Hofstadter, Douglas R. *Godel, Escher, Bach: An Eternal Golden Braid*. New York: Basic Books, 1999.

Holmgren, Stephen. *Ethics After Easter*. Cambridge, MA: Cowley Publications, 2000.

Hornwood, Sanford W. and I. Lucretia Hollingsworth, *Systematic Settlements: A Practical Guide for the Personal Injury Specialist*. The Lawyer's Cooperative Publishing Company: 1972.

Llich, John. *The Art and Skill of Successful Negotiation*.

Prentice-Hall, 1973.

Irvine, William B. *On Desire: Why We Want What We Want.* New York: Oxford University Press, 2006.

Jacker, Norbert S. *Effective Negotiation Techniques for Lawyers.* National Institute for Trial Advocacy, 1983.

Karass, Chester L. *Give and Take: The Complete Guide to Negotiating Strategies and Tactics.* Thomas Y. Crowell Company, 1974.

Keeva, Steven. "Opening the Mind's Eye" *ABA Journal* 82 (June, 1996), 48–57.

Kennedy, Gavin. *Essential Negotiation.* London: Profile Books Ltd, 2004.

Klein, Gary. *The Power of Intuition: How to Use Your Gut Feelings to Make Better Decisions at Work.* New York: Currency Doubleday, 2003.

Kramer, Henry S. *Game, Set, Match: Winning the Negotiation Game.* ALM Publishing/ALM Inc., 2001.

Krieger, Stefan H. and Richard K. Neumann. *Essential Lawyering Skills: Interviewing, Counseling, Negotiation, and Persuasive Fact Analysis.* Aspen Publishers, 2003.

Kronman, Anthony. *The Lost Lawyer: Failing Ideals of the Legal Profession.* Cambridge, MA: Harvard University Belknap Press, 2007.

Lax, David A. and James K. Sebenius. *3-D Negotiation: Powerful Tools to Change the Game in Your Most Important Deals.* Cambridge, MA: Harvard Business School Press, 2006.

______*The Manager as Negotiator.* Macmillan, 1986.

Lewicki, Litterer, Saunders, and Minton. *Negotiation: Readings, Exercises and Cases.* Irwin—McGraw Hill, 2nd Ed., 1993.

Levitt, Steven D. and Stephen J. Dubner. *Freakonomics: A Rogue Economist Explores the Hidden Side of Everything.* New York: HarperCollins Publishers, 2005.

Llyod, Robert M. "Hard Law Firm and Soft Law Schools." *North Carolina Law Review.* (March, 2005).

Manchester, William. *American Caesar: Douglas MacArthur 1880–1964.* New York: Dell, 1983.

McClendon, III., William H. "Louisiana's New Matrimonial Regime Law: Some Aspects of the Effect on Real Estate Practice." *Louisiana Law Review* 39, no. 2 (Winter, 1979), 441–77.

______"Negotiation Technique." *Louisiana Bar Journal.* 34 No. 6 (April, 1987), 338–342.

McNeilly, Mark R. *Sun Tzu and the Art of Business.* Original Translation by Samuel B. Griffith. New York: Oxford University Press, 2000.

Mehrabian, Albert. *Silent Messages: Implicit Communication of Emotions and Attitudes.* Wadsworth Publishing Company, 1980.

Mnookin, Robert H., Lawrence Susskind, and Pacey C. Foster. *Negotiating on Behalf of Others.* Sage Publications, 1999.

Mnookin, Robert H., Scott R. Peppet, and Andrew S. Tulumello. *Beyond Winning: Negotiating to Create Value in Deals and Disputes.* Cambridge, MA: Harvard University Press, 2000.

Murphy, James D. *Flawless Execution:Use the Techniques and Systems of America's Fighter Pilots to Perform at Your Peak and Win the Battles of the Business World.* New York: Regan Books, 2006.

Murphy, Kevin J. *Effective Listening: How to Profit by Tuning into the Ideas and Suggestions of Others.* Diane Publishing Company, 1992.

Murray, Donald M. *Learning by Teaching, Selected Articles in Writing and Teaching.* Portsmouth, NH, Boynton/Cook, 1982.

Nierenberg, Gerard I. *Fundamentals of Negotiation.* Hawthorne Books, 1968.

______*The Complete Negotiator.* Berkley Paperback Edition, 1991.

Nierenberg, Gerard I. and Henry H. Calero. *How To Read a Person Like A Book.* Pocket Books, 1973.

Nierenberg, Gerard I. and Henry H. Calero. *Meta-Talk: Guide to Hidden Meanings of Conversations.* Pocket Books, 1975.

Nouwen, Henri. *Return of the Prodigal: A Story of Homecoming.* New York: Doubleday/Image, 1994.

Overstreet, Stacy. "Excellence in Teaching." *Tulanian.* (Fall 2002).

Palmer, Parker J. *The Active Life: A Spirituality of Work, Creativity, and Caring.* San Francisco, CA: Jossey-Bass, 1999.

______*The Courage to Teach: Exploring the Inner Landscape of a Teacher's Life.* San Francisco, CA: Jossey-Bass, 1998.

Pasternak, David J. *Law Practice Management* (March 1998).

Peck, M. Scott. *The Road Less Traveled: A New Psychology of Love, Traditional Values and Spiritual Growth.* Touchstone, 2003.

Penick, Harvey. *Harvey Penick's Little Red Book: Lessons and Teachings from a Lifetime of Golf.* New York: Simon & Schuster, 1999.

Penick, Harvey and Bud Shrake. *And If You Play Golf, You're My Friend: Further Reflections of a Grown Caddie.* New York: Simon & Schuster, 1999.

Pink, Daniel H. *A Whole New Mind: Why Right-Brainers Will Rule the Future.* New York: Riverhead Books, 2006.

Pooley, Eric. "The Last Temptation of Al Gore." *Time.* (May 28, 2007).

Pruitt, Dean G. *Negotiation Behavior.* Academic Press, 1981.

Raiffa, Howard. *The Art and Science of Negotiation.* Harvard University Belknap Press, 1982.

Raiffa, Howard, John Richardson, and David Metcalfe. *Negotiation Analysis: The Science and Art of Collaborative Decision Making.* Cambridge, MA: Harvard University Press, 2003.

Reilly, Peter. "Teaching Law Students How to Feel: Using Negotiations Training to Increase Emotional Intelligence." *Negotiation Journal* 21. (April 2005), 301–314.

Rohn, James E. and Ronald L. Reynolds. *Seasons of Life.* Southlake, TX: Jim Rohn International, 1981.

Rosenthal Douglas E. *Lawyer and Client: Who's in Charge?* Russell Sage Foundation, 1974.

Sargent, Mark A. "What Does It Take? Hallmarks of the Business Lawyer." *Business Law Today* (July/August, 1996).

Sax, Leonard. *Why Gender Matters: What Parents and Teachers Need to Know about the Emerging Science of Sex Differences.* Broadway, 2006.

Schatzki, Michael and Wayne R. Coffey. *Negotiation: The Art of Getting What You Want.* Signet Paperback, 1981.

Schelling, Thomac C. *The Strategy of Conflict.* Oxford University Press, 1960.

Schumacher, E.F. *A Guide for the Perplexed.* New York: Harper Perennial, 1978.

Shaffer, Thomas L. and James R. Elkins. *Legal Interviewing and Counseling in a Nutshell.* 4th Ed. West, 2004.

Shea, Gordon F. *Creative Negotiating.* CBI Publishing Company, 1983.

Shell, G. Richard. *Bargaining for Advantage: Negotiation Strategies for Reasonable People*. Viking Penguin, 1999.

Shute, Nancy. "How Doctors Think." *U.S. News and World Report* (April 2, 2007).

Smith, Frank. *Understanding Reading: A Psycholinguistic Analysis of Reading and Learning to Read*. 6th Ed. TF-LEA, 2004.

Spence, Gerry. *How to Argue & Win Every Time: At Home, At Work, In Court, Everywhere, Everyday*. New York: St. Martin's Griffin, 1996.

Stone, Douglas, Bruce Patton, and Sheila Heen. *Difficult Conversations: How to Discuss What Matters Most*. Viking Penguin, 1999.

Svinicki, Marilla. *Learning and Motivation in the Postsecondary Classroom*. Bolton, MA: Anker Publishing Company, 2004.

Tannen, Deborah. *You Just Don't Understand: Women and Men in Conversation*. New York: HarperCollins, 2001.

Tejada-Flores, Lito. *Breakthrough on the New Skis: Say Goodbye to the Intermediate Blues*. 3rd Ed. Mountain Sports Press, 2001.

Teply, Larry L. *Legal Negotiation in a Nutshell*. West Publishing Company, 1991.

Tolstoy, Leo. *War and Peace*. New York: Viking, 2006.

Tournier, Paul. *The Strong and The Weak*. Translated by Edwin Hudson. Louisville, KY: Westminster John Knox Press, 1976.

Ury, William. *Getting Past No: Negotiating You Way From Confrontation to Cooperation*. Bantam Books, 1993.

Van Ginkel, Eric. "The Mediator as Face-Giver" *Negotiation Journal* 20 (October, 2004), 475–487.

Wagner, John Leo. "Aggressive ADR?" *Business Law Today* (May/June 1999).

Watkins, Michael H. *Shaping the Game: The New Leader's Guide to Effective Negotiating*. Cambridge, MA: Harvard Business School Press, 2006.

Williams, Gerald R. *Legal Negotiation and Settlement*. New York: West Publishing Company, 1983.

Yankelovich, Daniel. *The Magic of Dialogue: Transforming Conflict into Cooperation*. Touchstone, 2001.

Zander, Rosamund and Benjamin. *The Art of Possibility*. New York: Penguin Goup, 2002.

Zartman, I. William and Maureen Berman. *The Practical Negotiator.* New Haven, CT: Yale University Press, 1982.

Zuboff, Shoshana. "The Emperor's New Workplace" *Scientific American.* (September, 1995).

Zwicker, Milton W. "What Clients Really Want from their Lawyers." *Law Practice Management* (September, 1994).

Acknowledgments

I GRATEFULLY ACKNOWLEDGE THE CONTRIBUTIONS OF THOSE who have freely given of their time in supporting the evolution of this book. Special acknowledgments and thanks are due to my law partners and associates at Taylor Porter and Greg Bodin of Baker Donaldson, both in Baton Rouge, Louisiana; my wife, Genie; my four children, Hutch, Virginia, Eleanor, and Bryan, and their spouses, Prentiss Theus, Steve Harvin, Monte Bond, and Laura Howard; my talented legal assistants, Cathy Baker and Julia Guilbeau. And a personal note of special thanks is due to my late Mom and Pop for teaching me about timeless values.

Highest appreciation for subject design is due the late Judge Alvin B. Rubin of the United States Fifth Circuit Court of Appeals, who taught legal negotiations for many years at LSU and in 1986 gave me invaluable guidance and encouragement to re-offer this course with an innovative approach that focused on the connection between persuasion skills and professionalism.

Special thanks are due the Faculty Center for Excellence in Teaching and Learning at Western Carolina University and the Writing Center's director, Barbara Hardie, and associate director, Maryann Peterson, for suggestions in book organization. Graduate assistants at WCU have been outstanding, particularly, Jason Smith (Th.M., Harvard University), Kyle Ratsch, Eric Schilling, graduate student and graphic designer; Kiki Alimonos, Neal Piwowarski,

April Hicks, Cindy Goode Martin, and Josh Cole, assistants in the WCU Writing Center. I am very grateful to Stephany McFall for editing.

I also want to acknowledge the advice, insight, and encouragement of the following people: Professors Marsha Lee Baker, Reid Toth, John Slater, Howard and Jennifer Martin, Ruth Bennett, and Todd Eckerson; former Headmaster of Westminster School Don Werner; architect Fred Grace; banker Preston Wales; attorneys Leon Gary, Esq., Guy Lyman, Esq., Gordon F. Wilson, Jr. Esq.; editors Rick and Stephanie Harvin Nigel; the Reverend Jim Theus; seasoned business entrepreneurs Ed and Sally Ringle Hotchkiss, Jim and Nancy Wilkinson, John Graham, Tommy Maybanks; bookstore owner Donna B. Tucker; former president of The Citidel, General John Grinalds, former commandant of the U.S. Marine Corps, General Carl Mundy, and former Congressman Jack Edwards.

I am very grateful to journalist Jennifer Daniel of the Crossroads Chronicle for her composition suggestions and to Russell Majors and Lynda Simmons of Cashiers Printing for their expertise and patience in book printing; and to Steven Johannessen Design for cover artwork and layout. And I want especially to recognize editing suggestions and encouragement from M. Frank Woods, architect in London, England, Black Chaffe (Founder of Chaffe and Associates, New Orleans, LA), an engineer by training and experienced business negotiator in mergers and acquisitions, Dr. Edward J. Fox, Jr., Headmaster Emeritus Charlotte Latin School, and Hedy Okolichany, Administrative Assistant, Albert-Carlton Cashiers Community Library.

I also want to acknowledge Vice Chancellor Chaney Joseph of LSU Law School for asking me to teach at LSU in 1983, and Tom C. Galligan, former dean of the College of Law at the University of Tennessee for keen guidance when I taught at UT. I am very appreciative of the assistance from the staff at The University of Tennessee College of Law, especially the assistance of Sean Cary von Gunter, and from UT Professor Joan Heminway, who formerly practiced law with the firm Skadden, Arps, Slate, Meagher, & Flom, L.L.P., for editing comments. Gratitude also to my editor, Megan Welton, of Cedar Fort, Inc.

Special appreciation is due Professor George W. Kuney, Director of the University of Tennessee's Clayton Center for Entrepreneurial Law, for urging me to write *Deal Makers*.

Bill McClendon
Cashiers, North Carolina

November 2010

Index

About the
AUTHOR

Bill McClendon has practiced banking, real estate and commercial transaction law for almost fifty years with the firm of Taylor Porter in Baton Rouge, Louisiana. Prior to that, he was in the legal department of the Humble Oil & Refining Company in New Orleans and Houston. He has led seminars and taught both professional and graduate students at such distinguished institutions as the Banking School of the South, American Institute of Banking, Louisiana State University Law School, Western Carolina University (Assistant Professor in Business Law and part of the faculty of the graduate Engineering program), and the Clayton Center for Entrepreneurial Law at the University of Tennessee. A contributor to the Louisiana Law Review, Bill received the first Stephen T. Victory Memorial Reward for his article, Negotiation Techniques (Louisiana Bar Journal). He has also served as a professional mediator and arbitrator. He was educated at Newman School (New Orleans); Westminster School (Simsbury, Connecticut); The Leys (Cambridge, England) as an English-Speaking Union exchange scholar; Tulane University (New Orleans, Louisiana) where he earned a B.A. in History with one year in the MBA program and an L.L.B. in Law. Through the International House in New Orleans, he participated in a business exchange to San José, Costa Rica where he learned conversational Spanish. He is a Rotarian, an Advanced Toastmaster, a retired captain in the U.S. Army Reserve, and is listed in Who's Who in the World. Bill has four children and ten grandchildren for whom he is building a tree house. He enjoys hiking, gardening, woodworking, outdoor cooking, tennis, golf, and teaching adult-study classes in the Episcopal Church. A recipient of the 1997 Louisiana Historic Preservation Award, Bill, together with his wife, Genie, restored "Oakland at Gurley," an 1827 Carolina-type home and gardens in East Feliciana, Louisiana, and had it placed in the National Register of Historic Places. They presently reside in Cashiers, N.C. He serves as a facilitator in expanding right-brain thinking for the Board of Director of the Bascom Center for Visual Arts in Highlands, N.C.